LUCID DREAMS
IN 30 DAYS

Also by
Keith Harary
and
Pamela Weintraub

The 30-Day Altered States Series
Have an Out-of-Body Experience in 30 Days:
The Free Flight Program
Right Brain Learning in 30 Days:
The Whole Mind Program
Memory Enhancement in 30 Days:
The Total Recall Program
Mystical Experiences in 30 Days:
The Higher Consciousness Program
Inner Sex in 30 Days: The Erotic Fulfillment Program

Also by Keith Harary
Who Do You Think You Are? Explore Your Many-Sided Self
with the Berkeley Personality Profile

Also by Pamela Weintraub
Nurturing the Unborn Child: A Nine-Month Program for Soothing,
Stimulating,
and Communicating with Your Baby
The Complete Idiot's Guide to Surviving Divorce
You Can Save the Animals: 50 Things to Do Right Now
The Omni Interviews
Medical Emergency!: The St. Luke's-Roosevelt Hospital Center
Book of Emergency Medicine

LUCID DREAMS
IN 30 DAYS
THE CREATIVE SLEEP PROGRAM

Keith Harary, Ph.D.,
and
Pamela Weintraub

St. Martin's Griffin   New York

ISBN 0-312-19988-0

10 9 8 7 6

FOR THE DREAM YOGIS

CONTENTS

INTRODUCTION

Would you like to fly like Superman, traversing the globe to visit the Pyramids of Giza or a remote Tahitian beach? Do you crave a role in the next Spielberg blockbuster, complete with a million-dollar salary and an Academy Award? Would you like to talk cosmology with Stephen Hawking, live aboard the Space Station, or visit future cities on Mars? Whatever the fantasy, you can, with proper training and practice, learn to fulfill it in your dreams.

Most of the time, of course, you probably don't realize you've been dreaming until after you wake up. By then the dream has already come to an end. Some people, however, are conscious that they're dreaming while the dream is in progress. And, research now reveals, these lucid dreamers can direct their dreams, much like a film director directs a film. They can create or destroy characters, fly to distant locales, change their actions and the actions of others, even alter dream weather, scenery, or props.

To the uninitiated, such mental acrobatics may sound difficult, to say the least. But over the past two decades, researchers have documented the reality of lucid dreams and developed a series of simple lucid-dream exercises and techniques. These straightforward methods, presented step by step in the course of the Creative Sleep Program, should help make you the master of your dreams.

We think you'll find this special skill a commodity at the turn of the millennium, in our pragmatic, technologically challenging, and often-alienating world. These days we barely blink at the notion of relationships nurtured in cyberspace, and take for granted the cultural shift from psychotherapy to psychopharmacology as a treatment of choice. With less time to sleep, let alone dream, people spend endless hours in pursuit of material wealth; and then, for excitement, seek out prefabricated experiences that mimic real adventures of the past. The Explorers Club has never had more members, many of them seeking to retrace the routes of trailblazers who forged new territory a century back. The trend is no surprise. The pressures of twenty-first-century life have left us little time to journey inward. Yet the sophistication of our era has made it impossible to embrace the simplistic totems of inner exploration acceptable just a decade before. Few would resist the conclusion that the New Age movement, with its pyramid power, healing crystals, and mystical cults, seems hokey and quaint from the heights of 2000 A.D. With all we know of brain science, it's hard to buy into the notion that we can close our eyes and channel our ancestors, let alone the gods.

Yet millennial science has enabled a unique, over-the-edge, and authentic journey inward through the experience of the lucid dream. Thanks to breakthrough research into the techniques of lucid dreaming, you can explore your deepest inner realm without ever turning on a computer or venturing from home. While the Yogis of Tibet have reported lucid dream states for thousands of years, modern science began its intensive study of the field only in the 1970s. The work has paid off.

Today, laboratory researchers at Stanford University and elsewhere have charted the psychophysiology of this unique state of consciousness, providing a road map for those who would like to experience it for themselves. Physiological measurements, for instance, show that dreams of singing, counting, and even making love affect the dreamer's brain, and to a lesser extent, the body, much as these same experiences do in real life. Researchers know that specific techniques, including whirling or rubbing hands together during a dream, can prolong the experience—though the studies show whirling is best if you'd like to change venues, while rubbing is most effective for keeping the backdrop the same. Laboratory science has even developed a means of communicating with lucid dreamers during the dream.

Thanks to such research, you'll find the exercises presented in this book especially effective. In fact, by the end of our four-week program you should be able to induce and sustain lucid dreams, fly to distant dream locales, take part in crafted, extraordinary dream adventures, explore your most private sexual fantasies with a variety of dream lovers, investigate creative solutions to personal and professional problems, and even boost your immune system to enhance your health. You may also find yourself transcending ordinary perceptions of reality as you come to terms with your innermost thoughts and feelings about death, existentialism, and God. As a bonus, Creative Sleep participants will learn our own method for inducing an especially intense form of the lucid-dream experience—an altered state we call high lucidity, based on principles originally put forth centuries ago by Yogis in Tibet.

Before you begin, we'd like you to think of dreaming in much the same way you think of driving a car. Remember all the times you've driven along the highway seemingly not paying attention at all. All of a sudden you've looked at the road and realized that someone has been exerting judgment and control—and that someone you've recognized in a flash is you. Dreaming works in a similar way. You usually aren't consciously aware of your ability to control the action; but of course, right down to the exact words spoken by your dream characters, the very last brick in your dream house, and the precise number of petals on a flower in your dream garden, you alone are the author and designer of your dreams. Realizing this fact is much like suddenly realizing that you are driving the car. Waking up in your dreams, in other words, requires a subtle shift in attention, so that you learn to be more completely aware of what you're doing.

In Week One of the Creative Sleep Program this subtle shift of attention will begin. You will learn basic techniques for recalling and recording your dreams. You will also learn to tune into the difference between waking consciousness and dream sleep. Finally, Week One exercises should bring you to the brink of dream consciousness, teaching you to predetermine dream subjects and even seize a small amount of control while you dream.

Weeks Two and Three will teach you how to have and control full-blown lucid dreams. As you practice the exercises within these chapters, you should become increasingly adept at dream flying, which can enable you to navigate your dream terrain; dream whirling, which can help you sustain your lucid dreams; and dream weaving, the art of manipulating the details in your dreams. As you advance from ordinary lucid dreaming to the more acutely alert state of high lucidity, the intensity and power of your lucid dream experiences should increase.

Finally, in Week Four, you will learn how to develop creative consciousness, in which you can use your virtuoso skills to explore the farther reaches of your lucid-dream potential. After all, if lucid dreaming merely enabled you to convert dream apples to oranges or experience flying to the Arctic, it would be a limited skill. The most experienced lucid dreamers therefore use their abilities not so much to change the dream landscape as to explore it. In this way, one may conduct regular expeditions into the outback of one's own subconscious without a psychotherapist or drugs.

Please remember, in the long run, lucid and high-lucid dreaming should be viewed as an opportunity to get in touch with an expansive inner realm. Indeed, anyone who constantly directs dream characters and alters dream props without trying to explore their deeper symbolic meaning may ultimately suppress their subconscious needs rather than allowing them to find expression.

In an effort to offset such potential difficulties, we recommend that you balance controlled lucid dreaming with free dreaming (dreaming that is not in any way consciously controlled). We include two nights of free dreaming in the Creative Sleep Program, and we also recommend that you integrate this sort of balanced approach into any long-term exploration of lucid dreaming you may decide to pursue. The best way to master lucid dreaming is one step at a time. Give yourself time to focus on each of the Creative Sleep exercises, and don't rush it. Although the program is designed to be carried out in thirty days, don't feel constrained by this if you prefer to take longer.

We do not recommend completing the program in less than thirty days, however, or trying to squeeze an entire week's worth of exercises into a single weekend. Although many of the Creative Sleep exercises are conceptually quite simple, their combined impact could be profound. We recommend that you allow your abilities to evolve gradually, giving you an opportunity to adjust. Moreover, since dreams, be they ordinary dreams or lucid ones, reflect your current mood, a balanced approach should increase the enjoyment and overall scope of your nocturnal adventures. Indeed, the best way to approach lucid dreaming is by not pressuring yourself to have lucid dreams. If you feel a sense of anxiety about having these dreams, they will be less likely to occur. Remember, lucid dreams may emerge at any point in the Creative Sleep Program; lucid dreaming is not, after all, a strictly linear process in which the goal is reached or not reached at the end of every exercise. Rather, this program interacts in an ongoing fashion with each individual user, helping to set the appropriate conditions for lucid and high-lucid dreams. But the exact timetable you'll follow is really up to you and your personal predisposition. Lucid dreams may begin right away for some, later on in the program for others, and after the program has been completed for others still.

We want to emphasize that it would be most unusual for anyone to report problems as a result of the Creative Sleep Program, especially since the program does not attempt to replace psychotherapy in any way, shape, or form. However, if you have a history of emotional or psychiatric problems, or if you feel at all uncomfortable about any of the exercises, we suggest you check with your therapist or psychiatrist before proceeding. In such a case, you might wish to carry out the Creative Sleep Program only under his or her continued clinical guidance.

No matter who you are, the Creative Sleep Program has been designed for your enjoyment. As you gain experience, your lucid dreams should become increasingly vivid and powerful. They should also give you greater access to the hidden stores of energy, wisdom, and experience you've gained in the course of your life.

WEEK ONE

WAKING UP TO YOUR DREAMS

WEEK ONE

•

WAKING UP TO YOUR DREAMS

Most of us think of the everyday world as fairly concrete and predictable. Dreams, on the other hand, are considered fantasies, changeable mirages that can dissolve in a mist. Yet the waking world is filled with unpredictable, bizarre, surrealistic images, including freakish crimes and stunning works of art that seem the stuff of dreams. Dreams, on the other hand, contain the deepest truth about our unconscious thoughts toward reality. If we could only grasp the meaning of our dreams, we would understand our relationship with other people and the world around us with far more precision and depth.

In fact, dream sleep and alert wakefulness are just two states along the continuum of consciousness we experience every day. During most dreams we experience ourselves as awake, and sometimes while awake we may wonder if we're really in a dream. It stands to reason, therefore, that if we are ever to wake up in our dreams—to become lucid—we must learn to differentiate the dream state and the waking state in a sure and powerful way.

Week One of the Creative Sleep Program helps you achieve this goal by teaching you to keenly observe the nature of waking reality and the nature of dreams. In the first part of the week, you will learn to recall your dreams and record them in a dream journal. You will also learn to immerse yourself in the surrealistic images that haunt waking reality, often giving it many of the subjective qualities of a dream.

Week One exercises also introduce some of the basic tenets of dream control. You will, for instance, create a sleeping

3

environment conducive to more conscious dreaming. You will learn how to influence the general subject matter of your dreams through a process known as dream incubation. And you will even learn an effective approach to problem solving; focus on an issue in your life using the technique described in Week One, and a solution may well appear in your dreams.

Finally, by confronting the negative images that sometimes emerge in your dreams, you will learn how to move through your discomfort to a state of semi-awareness. As you develop the ability to interrogate your dream enemies, a veil will start to lift. You will start to wake up in your dreams.

One important note: though Week One techniques are intended to serve as a prelude to lucid dreaming, they are valuable tools in and of themselves. Indeed, even if one never has a lucid dream, keeping a dream journal can provide a basis for deep exploration of the inner self. Incubating dreams on creative and romantic dilemmas can provide valuable avenues for professional and personal insight and success. And examining or interrogating fearful dream images so you can come to better understand them may help eliminate recurring dreams and even nightmares.

Please do not underestimate the importance of Week One techniques to the rest of the Creative Sleep Program. They form the bedrock upon which the upcoming weeks of lucid dreaming are based.

DAYS 1 AND 2

DREAM RECALL

Before you can become conscious in your dreams, you must master some basic tenets of dream control. A major requirement for successful dream control is the ability to remember, appreciate, and record your dreams. On Days 1 and 2 of the Creative Sleep Program, therefore, you will learn special focusing exercises to help you recall your dreams. You will also learn to record your dreams in your private dream journal.

> **Dream Alert**—Because some preparation is required, read all the instructions for Days 1 and 2 before you begin.

Part I: Setting Up Your Dream Journal.

Your first task, to be carried out on Day 1, is preparation of the dream journal you will use for the rest of the Creative Sleep Program. Your personal dream journal should be a notebook that you can store under your pillow or carry around during the day. We suggest *Dreams and Waking Visions* by Mary Michael and Barbara Andrews, or an easy-to-carry spiral memo book. You should also select a special pen for your dream journal. We suggest a free-flowing felt-tip pen that will enable you to write while lying down. The pen used for writing in your dream journal should not be used for anything else. You may also find it helpful to clip a penlight to your dream journal, in case you find yourself remembering a dream in the middle of the night.

Take your new journal home and place it, along with the pen and penlight, under the pillow on your bed. Say to yourself, *This is where I'll be recording my remembered dreams.* Then leave the notebook under your pillow until you're ready to go to bed.

Part II: Remembering Your Dreams.

The second part of the dream recall exercise can begin anytime after you've set up your dream journal. It will begin on Day 1 and continue through the morning of Day 2.

Begin by sitting alone in a public place during some quiet part of your day and observing yourself and your surroundings. Observe the other people around you and repeat these words: *Everybody here has dreams.* Consider the meaning of this phrase and try to imagine what the various people around you might have dreamed last night. Consider your current surroundings and ask yourself what they might dream tonight. What might *you* dream tonight?

Then, quietly say to yourself, *From now on, I'll remember my dreams.* As soon as you acknowledge your willingness to remember your dreams, let go of the whole idea and forget about it for the rest of the day, until you're lying in bed, drifting off to sleep.

> **Dream Alert**—If you feel particularly ambitious, you may suggest to yourself that you wake up throughout the night as you complete your dreams. With continued practice, you may find yourself waking after quite a number of successive dreams on a particular night and remembering each of them. While you might not wish to practice such an intense exercise on a regular basis, it can occasionally lead to some surprising insights, while also significantly increasing your ability to recall your dreams.

Later, after you've gone to bed, gently reaffirm your willingness to remember your dreams. Once again, let go of this thought the moment that you acknowledge it, and avoid putting any psychological pressure on yourself. Then fall asleep.

To retain your dreams as completely as possible, you must first understand that dream memories can be as fleeting as your next breath of air. Therefore, whenever you start to wake up, be it in the middle of the night or first thing in the morning, do not open your eyes or even move. Instead, stop and focus entirely on recalling your dreams.

Toward this end, you must arrange your sleeping environment to avoid even the tiniest distractions. If you usually sleep with or near another person, ask them not to disturb you before you get out of bed in the morning. If you usually wake up with the aid of an alarm clock, we suggest that you use a clock radio and set it to wake you with classical music instead of a buzzer. Better yet, arrange for a friend or family member to gently rouse you from sleep.

Don't pressure yourself to remember detailed and convoluted dream descriptions in exact chronological order. As you have probably found when trying to recapture other memories, such as the title of some forgotten song, dream memories are best approached with subtlety and grace. They must be allowed to steep, to emerge gradually and spontaneously into your conscious waking awareness.

You are most likely to remember details or fragments of your most *recent* dream upon first awakening. The thoughts, feelings, and images pertaining to this dream can often be gently followed in reverse order, gradually guiding you back toward subtle recollections of earlier dreams.

Recollections of earlier dreams, however, are typically as fragile and fleeting as soap bubbles. These dreams, after all, are composed of feelings and images gently blowing through the hidden passages of your unconscious mind. Any sudden movement in your thoughts, any momentary distraction, any attempt to force the memory can shatter the bubbles and cause the images to evaporate before they emerge in your conscious awareness.

Remember, you must relax, and most important, you must give yourself time to remember your dreams. If dream images don't instantly float to the surface of your conscious awareness, just lie quietly for a while and see what happens before turning your attention toward anything else that may be on your mind.

Part III: Recording Your Dreams.   Dream journals have been kept in one form or another throughout recorded history. Though we cannot absolutely prove the theory, we would be willing to bet that even cave paintings created by the earliest human beings have at least occasionally represented images that first emerged in dreams.

As civilization evolved, dream journals took the form of written records detailing and analyzing the dreamer's nightly experiences. Most modern dream researchers view this personal written record as an effective means of facilitating dream recall and keeping track of dream themes and images.

To keep your dream journal, give each dream a title as you record it. Make sure that you always record the date and approximate time of your dream. For each particular night, keep track of which dreams you had earlier in the sleep cycle, and which you had later on. As you write, be sure to note the setting or settings in which each dream occurred, the characters who appeared in the dream, any significant props or symbols that stand out in your mind, and any emotions that the dream may have triggered in you. We also strongly recommend that you use your dream journal to explore the relationship between your dreams and your daily concerns and activities. Please leave one or two blank pages after each dream entry, so that you can add any additional thoughts, recollections, or interpretations that may occur to you as time goes on.

Although it is not mandatory, feel free to draw any pictures that relate to your dreams. Visual images can express the underlying meaning of a dream in graphic form and may even trigger the release of deeper memories.

Beginning the morning of Day 2, you must get into the habit of writing down your dream descriptions after just waking up, before you even get out of bed. The longer you wait, the more likely these memories are to become distorted or to simply fade.

Treat your dream journal as a sacred book in which you record and interpret the innermost creations of your unconscious mind. For at least the next three and a half weeks of the Creative Sleep Program, try to keep your journal with you at all times. You may recall a dream any time during the day; there is no time limit on the flashes of insight you are likely to have once you've initiated the dream recall process upon first waking up in the morning.

> **Dream Alert**—Since dream recall can dramatically improve with practice, we urge you to carry out the most crucial aspects of Days 1 and 2 through the remainder of the Creative Sleep Program. First of all, just as you're falling asleep each evening, quietly affirm to yourself in your thoughts that you intend to remember your dreams when you first wake up. Second, allow yourself time as often as possible to remember and reflect on your dream experiences upon awakening, before you open your eyes, move, or concern yourself with any other thoughts. Third, conscientiously use your dream journal to record your dreams.

WALDEN POND BOOKS
3316 GRAND AVENUE
OAKLAND, CA 94610
510-832-4438
Exchanges Only w/ rcpt. 10days

30-Nov-05   12:59 PM
Clerk: user02 Register # 2

Trans. #151307
        * - Non Taxable Items

0312199880   1 $9.95 $9.95
 LUCID DREAMS IN 30 DAYS
1400032903   1 $13.95 $13.95
 BANGKOK 8
Total Items: 2
            Sub-Total: $23.90
            Tax @ 8.750%: $2.09
               Total: $25.99
        Total Tendered: $40.00
           Change Due: ($14.01)

Payment Via:
   CASH $40.00
   Change (Cash)   ($14.01)

NO REFUNDS/EXCHANGES ON CDS/USED BOOKS

DAY 3

TEMPLE OF
DREAMS

On Day 3 you will learn to influence your dreams through the thoughts and images you have just before falling asleep. This potent technique, known as *dream incubation,* has been practiced all over the world in one form or another since ancient times.

Dream incubation may be as complex as spending days in a special environment meditating and practicing elaborate cultural rituals, or it may be as simple as quietly telling yourself to dream about a certain topic just before falling asleep. The dream incubation technique we have created for the Creative Sleep Program is simple and effective and should provide you with increasingly greater control over your dreams. As you apply this technique throughout the program, you should find it a potent tool for solving problems, changing bad habits, boosting your immune system, and getting to know your deepest self.

The first part of our dream incubation process involves sanctifying your dream environment—imbuing your regular sleeping habitat with an emotional ambience conducive to the induction of desired dreams.

Begin Day 3, therefore, by reflecting on the psychological atmosphere of your usual sleep environment. Consider the possible influence that any objects or images within this setting may have on your dreams. Are your immediate sleep surroundings rich in stimulating and nurturing images, such as works of art and pictures of your loved ones? Or is your bedroom sterile, marked by stark visual images and piles of paperwork you've brought home from the office? Do you sleep and dream in generally quiet surroundings, or is the atmosphere frequently jarred by traffic noise or the sound of a television in another room? Is the usual temperature of your sleep environment comfortable? Is the ventilation adequate? Is the color of your room soothing to your spirit, or do you find it overstimulating or just plain boring? Most important, what emotional messages do you receive from your sleep environment? What does that environment say about your personal relationships and values, and what does it reflect about your attitudes toward sleep and dreaming?

Once you have considered the issues above, make your dream room as calm and comfortable as possible. Decorate it with favorite objects that express the most positive aspects of your personality. Do your best to make the room attractive, and remove any disturbing or intrusive images that might interfere with dream exploration.

After you have created a dream sanctuary in the privacy of your home, sit in that consecrated spot and focus on a matter of personal concern about which you would like to dream. Choose a situation over which you have direct influence, such as your behavior toward your mother-in-law, or your response to some pressing situation in your private or professional life. Be specific. The more precisely you express the matter of concern before you fall asleep, the more specific the subsequent dream is likely to be.

> **Dream Alert**—For this initial exercise, we urge you not to focus on potentially life-changing or traumatic personal concerns, such as, *Should I get married?* Until you gain experience, intense feelings might unconsciously prevent you from having a particular dream or from recalling a dream you have successfully induced. At the same time, your chosen subject should be significant enough to motivate your unconscious mind to produce the corresponding dream. We therefore recommend avoiding such psychologically trivial concerns as, *Should I change the brand of cat litter I've been using?*

Once you've decided on an appropriate and meaningful topic, it's time to induce a relevant dream. First, place your dream journal, special pen, and penlight in a prominent spot beside the bed. Then carefully select one or more symbolic objects that reflect the underlying mood and focus of your intended dream. If you want to induce a dream about the advisability of accepting a recent job offer at the circus, for example, you might select a clown doll for your symbolic object, along with a box of Cracker Jacks and a picture of some baby elephants. If you're exploring your unconscious feelings about your relationship with some individual, you might select some pictures and objects that remind you of that particular person and any memorable experiences you've had together.

As you select these objects, focus on the subject of your intended dream, gently excluding all other thoughts from your mind. Calmly tell yourself that you expect to dream about the matter of concern, and that you'll remember the dream when you awaken.

Once you've selected the appropriate dream incubation objects, carefully arrange them in an aesthetically interesting fashion within your special dream room. You may even place one or more of these objects in bed with you, if you wish. You may also enhance the atmosphere by burning incense or playing music particularly conducive to the intended subject matter of your incubated dream.

Just before you turn off the light for the night and go to sleep, take a few moments to follow the "phrase focusing" technique developed by San Francisco dream psychologist Gayle Delaney and based upon a suggestion originally made by psychologist Carl Jung: articulate the topic of your prospective dream in a single sentence, such as, *Should I accept the job offer at Ringling Brothers?* or *How do I really feel about Melvin?* Then, using your special pen, write the phrase in your dream journal. If you wish, you might also draw a picture to illustrate the issue at hand. As soon as you're finished, turn off the light and go to sleep.

Continue focusing on your phrase and/or picture. As you fall asleep, picture the special objects you've placed around you in the room. Quietly remind yourself to dream about the subject at hand and to gain insights into your unconscious feelings toward it while you sleep. Remind yourself also that you will remember all related dreams when you wake up.

Dream Alert—When you wake up, remember to practice the dream recollection techniques you learned on Day 2. Before moving or opening your eyes, concentrate on recalling your most recent dream. Follow these thoughts back to earlier images and dreams. Record any dreams in your journal immediately after opening your eyes.

Finally, to see if this exercise has been truly helpful, study any pictures, phrases, or questions you recorded in your dream journal before going to sleep. Explore the possible relationship between these and your actual dreams.

DAY 4

VISION QUEST

On Day 4 you will use dream incubation to gain further influence over your dreams. This time you will focus on inducing a dream that taps your creative abilities, helping you to come up with a new idea or an innovative approach to life.

Begin by reflecting on your general creative needs. If you are a grade school teacher, note that you'd like to present letters and numbers in a more interesting and innovative way. If you program computers, acknowledge that the software you work with could be simpler to use.

Now pick a particular creative need that is of some pressing concern. Perhaps you're a writer, trying to come up with a lead for your latest magazine article. Perhaps you are a detective trying to figure out how an anonymous note can help trap a murderer. You may be an artist seeking inspiration for a painting or work of sculpture, a business executive searching for a way to close a deal, or even a doctor trying to figure out what's really wrong with a patient.

If the matter is of serious concern to you, then on some level you've most likely already been thinking about it. In fact, given your personal background, you probably already possess some subtle, perhaps unconscious clues to the answer you are seeking. All you must really do, then, is go on a *vision quest*—

that is, allow your experience, knowledge, and creative energy to merge in a moment of intuitive vision that expresses itself in a dream.

Spend some time during the day allowing your thoughts to roam freely over your creative dilemma. Calmly tell yourself you will express a solution in your dreams. Then, just as you did yesterday, gather some objects that remind you of the issue at hand and place them around your sleeping environment.

Just before going to sleep, create a phrase or doodle that best expresses your problem, and enter it on a fresh page in your dream journal. Continue focusing on this phrase or doodle as you drift off to sleep. Tell yourself that you will have a relevant dream and will remember it immediately upon awakening.

Remember to practice dream recollection techniques when you first wake up, and to write down any and all impressions of your remembered dreams as quickly as possible. You may be surprised to find yourself dreaming about specific images, words, ideas, or metaphors that relate to your creative concerns in a powerful way. You may even wake up with an apparent solution, whether or not you can relate this inspiration to a specific dream.

Remember, creative ideas or images that emerge from incubated dreams must be evaluated from the perspective of rational, waking consciousness. You may find yourself initially inspired by your dream vision, only to realize later in the day that it requires further development. On the other hand, especially if you practice creative dream incubation on a regular basis, you may be delighted to find yourself reaching full waking awareness with a completely formed and coherent mental image, idea, or impression that is directly applicable to your immediate creative needs.

As you progress through the Creative Sleep Program, you may find that simple dream incubation regularly helps you solve personal problems, improve your health, or enhance your career. Most important, however, dream incubation techniques should take you a long way toward communicating with the inner part of yourself accessible primarily through your dreams. Once this communication has been established, you will be better able to negotiate the surrealistic and compelling terrain of lucid, or conscious, sleep.

DAY 5

LIFE IS BUT A
DREAM

Using dream incubation, you can deftly influence the subject matter of your dreams beforehand; nonetheless, once the dream has started, you lack active control. On Day 5, therefore, you will take the Creative Sleep Program one step further by practicing some of the skills you'll need if you are to truly wake up in your dreams.

The first step in this process is a detailed exploration of waking reality, which you must learn to differentiate from dreams. On the face of it, of course, waking reality seems vastly different from the world of dreams. But in many ways dream sleep and total wakefulness are just two of the states along the continuum of consciousness you experience every day. For instance, you might be fully awake in the morning, daydream in the afternoon, and enter a hypnagogic state, characterized by vivid but conscious imagery, in the late evening as you're falling asleep. Then, throughout the night, you sleep and dream. Given all this, it's our feeling that greater awareness of the waking world will enhance your sensitivity to the full spectrum of inner states, including your dreams.

To begin, choose a nearby location reminiscent of some of the scenes you've seen in your dreams. Depending upon your dreams, a beautiful cathedral, a peaceful suburban street, a busy train station, a sculpture garden, a café, or the roof of a building overlooking a neon sign at night might serve you well. If at all possible, the place you choose should be vibrant and evocative, capable of stimulating *all* your senses. Most important, it should present you with images that seem as dreamlike and surreal as possible.

> **Dream Alert**—Before you read any further, go to the location you've chosen for Day 5. When you arrive, sit down and carefully absorb the instructions below.

Since you're reading this paragraph, we'll assume that you are now in the middle of some interesting, dreamlike locale. Look around at the spot you've chosen. Notice exactly where you are in relation to everything and everyone around you. Take it all in, giving yourself plenty of time to completely absorb the aesthetic and emotional impact of your surroundings.

Then, consider the fact that the place you have chosen is a reflection of your own personality and imagination. Out of all the possible places available to you for this exercise, this is the one that you decided to select, right down to the very spot in which you are sitting now. In other words, your current surroundings reflect your personal and subjective approach to everyday reality.

Did you choose one of the places we suggested or come up with a place of your own? Did you choose a place you've been before, or someplace totally unfamiliar?

Now, as you look around, ask yourself the following question: *What is it about this place that reminds me of my dreams?*

To find the answer within yourself, reflect on the nature of your dreams. Have you ever dreamed about this place? If you were dreaming about this place right now, what might you expect to happen next?

Observe the other people in your immediate surroundings. As you watch them, say to yourself in your thoughts, *Everybody here has dreams*.

In fact, consider the possibility that those around you have at some point also dreamed about this place. Some of you have probably known this place in two separate realities: the waking world and the world of dreams. Indeed, how many of the buildings, products, and artifacts around you were inspired by unconscious images while some creative individuals were asleep and dreaming? Could your experience of waking reality, including everything from the street you live on to the music you love, be, on some level at least, a conscious expression of images from your own and other people's dreams?

Now get up and walk around the area you have selected for ten or fifteen minutes. As you walk, notice possible dream images all around you.

> **Dream Alert**—After you have finished this exercise, go about the rest of the day in your usual fashion. Before going to bed at night, read the instructions for Day 6.

> **Dream Alert**—Now that you have become a dream observer of the waking world, continue to look for images that may have been inspired by dreams. You may find such images in architecture, advertising, movies, music, art, science, and literature, among other places. From now on, whenever you notice a particularly compelling collection of dreamlike images, say to yourself, *I may dream about these images sometime in the future.* Then let the thought go as soon as you recognize and acknowledge this possibility.

DAY 6

DREAM
REHEARSAL

On Day 6 of the Creative Sleep Program you will continue your journey toward greater conscious awareness in your dreams. The goal of today's exercise: creating and acting out a "dream" while you are still awake. Consider this dress rehearsal a practice run. By creating a dream script, and then consciously altering it as you go, you will actually be simulating a lucid dream. The simulation should help you feel more comfortable about the notion of waking up in your dreams.

Begin the dream rehearsal exercise the moment you wake up in the morning, before you open your eyes or even move. As you're preparing to confront the waking world, tell yourself in your thoughts, *I am going to sleep.* Then wake up and go about your day, but continue to tell yourself that the waking world is actually a dream.

The next part of this exercise calls for some creativity: you must prepare a script for the dream you will later rehearse. To create your script, you might first recall some particularly striking dream you've had in the past. If you can't remember a specific dream, create a script from images and thoughts that fit into your general idea of a dream. Remember, your goal here is not to precisely capture your real dreams, nor is it to create a simulated dream that makes complete psychological sense. Rather, you should strive to immerse yourself in sensations and impressions that give you the *feeling* of a dream. For instance, you might script a dream in which you are lost in a strange city without any money or friends. Alternatively, you might script a dream in which you are one of the Ghostbusters, toting a proton pack and aching to bust some ghosts.

The dream you come up with should be one you can readily act out while awake. Please make sure the setting is safe and accessible. If your dream rehearsal calls for a coactor, please feel free to enlist the participation of an understanding friend or partner. You can even surprise each other with some unexpected dreamlike actions, conversations, and responses throughout the dream simulation.

Before going to the place you've chosen, dress up in a way that suits the emotional atmosphere and imagery of a dream. For example, you may wear something you don't usually wear everyday, and which might even seem a bit out of place for the setting you've selected. Try wearing a formal dress or dinner jacket to a casual gathering of friends, layers of garish costume jewelry to a company picnic, or furry red bedroom slippers for a stroll through your local downtown shopping district.

Once you have selected a suitable setting for this exercise and have dressed appropriately—or inappropriately—for the occasion, it's time to carry out your waking dream. Begin by telling yourself that you are actually fast asleep and dreaming. Then, as you follow through with your dream script, pay attention to the input of all your senses. Also note the emotional quality of your dream simulation experience. Feel free to act spontaneously, rewriting some of the script as you go along. Allow imagery and experiences to emerge from your unconscious. Then change them at will to suit your insights and desires, much as you might in a real lucid dream.

At some point during this exercise you should actually ask yourself whether or not you're dreaming. Take a few moments to calmly consider the meaning of this question, and imagine that you're really at home in bed sleeping. Then respond affirmatively, answering, *Yes, this entire experience is a dream.*

As you complete your simulated dream activity, quietly say to yourself in your passing thoughts, *I may dream about this entire experience later.* As soon as you acknowledge this thought, let go of it. Then continue with the rest of your normal daily activities.

Complete your dream rehearsal exercise later, after you go to bed. As you're on the verge of falling asleep, tell yourself that you are actually on the verge of waking up and becoming fully conscious and alert. Say to yourself in your thoughts, *Soon I will be wide awake in my dreams and consciously aware of everything that's happening.* Then allow yourself to drift off into deep sleep.

> **Dream Alert**—We recommend that from now on, whenever you encounter a particularly extraordinary dreamlike or surrealistic set of images or experiences, you take a moment to ask yourself in your thoughts if you're awake or dreaming. Consider the question seriously before answering it. Though you'll often be awake when you ask yourself this question, you may also be surprised at some point to discover that you really are home in bed, having a lucid dream.

DAY 7

EDGE OF
CONSCIOUSNESS

If all goes well, Day 7 will bring you to the edge of dream consciousness. To get there, you must learn to confront and explore the negative or unpleasant images that often appear in dreams. Such images, because they can be quite powerful, usually trigger a level of conscious arousal that results in the termination of a given dream. (You may have noticed, for example, that nightmares often trigger a sudden awakening.) However, by focusing upon these powerful dream images and learning to approach them with curiosity rather than fear, you can actually achieve a higher level of dream awareness without returning to full waking consciousness. An additional benefit, of course, is that understanding scary or just plain unpleasant dream images may help you resolve problems that have seemed particularly entrenched.

To achieve a greater level of wakefulness in your dreams, perhaps purging some inner demons in the process, wake up on the morning of Day 7 and tell yourself that you'll consciously confront and examine all negative images inhabiting your dreams. As you go about your day, think of negative images that have haunted your dreams in the past. As these images float by in your thoughts, tell them you intend to discover the secrets they conceal. *After all,* you might tell them, *I created you to express something to my unconscious mind, and if you don't cooperate with me, I can destroy and replace you with something else.*

At night, before you go to bed, retire to your dream environment. Choose an image or object that reminds you of tonight's special goal and place it in the room where you sleep. This incubation symbol should be something that reminds you of a hostile or negative image you've encountered in a past dream. Using your special pen, write these words in your dream journal: *Tonight I'll explore the meaning of hostile images in my dreams by confronting them and asking that they explain themselves.* Then turn off the light and go to sleep.

As you drift off to sleep, think back on some of the negative dream images you've encountered in the past. Commit yourself to confronting these images or others like them, and strive to become as consciously aware of this activity as possible within the dream.

When you do encounter a hostile dream image, do your best to remind yourself that the image is a creation of your own mind. You will very likely find that the intensity of this confrontation increases your general level of self-awareness, perhaps even motivating the kind of automatic fight or flight response than can stimulate a sudden escape to waking reality. It is essential, for the purposes of this exercise, that you do your best within the dream to quell this reaction. Instead of running away, or confronting your dream adversary head-on, use your increased level of awareness to calmly claim your personal power. Turn to the hostile dream image and ask it what it really wants from you. (It's interesting to note that some dreamers actually try to destroy their dream enemies; however, as any student of Freud might guess, this technique often obliterates the nightmare but not the problem, which continues to fester in other forms.)

Especially when first practicing this exercise, it is natural to find yourself returning to waking consciousness early in the dream. If you do begin to wake up in response to a threatening dream, you should, if possible, continue lying in bed while maintaining a state of semiconsciousness. In this state between wakefulness and sleep, concentrate on confronting and interrogating any negative dream images in your half waking thoughts. This process can still lead you toward a better understanding of your negative dream images, even though you are not actually dreaming at the time, because in such a state you should have increased access to your unconscious mind. In Week Two, you will learn how to follow this semiconscious state of dream awareness backward into sleep and a fully lucid dream.

Dream Alert—Don't forget to record all your dreams in your dream journal. If you gain insight into a hidden part of yourself through a dream experience, remember to record your insight along with the dream. Remember, also, if you are at all uncomfortable about exploring the meaning of your dreams on your own, feel free to seek the counsel of a competent therapist.

WEEK ONE   WAKING UP TO YOUR DREAMS

DAY 1 DREAM RECALL	**DAY 2** DREAM RECALL	**DAY 3** TEMPLE OF DREAMS		
Buy a notebook, a felt-tip pen, and a penlight. Place notebook, pen, and penlight under your pillow. Observe the world around you. As you go to bed at night, vow to remember your dreams. Go to sleep.	Upon waking up in the morning, lie quietly in bed and let dream images come to you. Give each remembered dream a title, and record details verbally or pictorially. Carry your dream journal with you throughout the day to record any additional details that emerge. Before you go to bed at night, vow to remember your dreams.	In the morning, recall and record your dreams. Study your usual sleep environment. Make your sleep environment as calm and comfortable as possible. Sit in your sleep environment and focus on a matter of personal concern about which you would like to dream. Place dream journal and pen on bed. Select objects that symbolize your intended dream.	Write the topic of your intended dream in your dream journal, repeating it in your mind as you fall asleep.	

DAY 4 VISION QUEST	DAY 5 LIFE IS BUT A DREAM	DAY 6 DREAM REHEARSAL	DAY 7 EDGE OF CONSCIOUS- NESS
In the morning, recall and record your dreams. Reflect on a serious creative need. Express your creative dilemma in your dream journal before going to bed. Before you fall asleep, vow to remember your dreams.	In the morning, recall and record your dreams. Choose a nearby, dreamlike location in the real world and spend part of your day there observing the scenery and action. Read instructions for Day 6. Before you go to bed, vow to recall your dreams.	Upon awakening, before you open your eyes, tell yourself that you are falling asleep. Recall your dreams. Get up and record your dreams. Prepare a dream script. Act out the dream script sometime during the day. Go to bed, and as you're on the verge of falling asleep, tell yourself that you are actually waking up.	In the morning, recall and record your dreams. During the day tell yourself you will consciously examine negative images the next time you dream. Choose an appropriate symbol to place in your dream room and write your intention in your dream journal. Focus on your goal as you drift off to sleep. In your dreams, ask unpleasant images and entities what they mean to you.

WEEK TWO

LUCID DREAMING

WEEK TWO

•

L U C I D   D R E A M I N G

*I*n Week Two you will learn the core techniques for the Creative Sleep Program: how to enter, sustain, and influence the course of a lucid dream. Essentially, the techniques described in this chapter teach you how to take a dream already in progress and render it lucid through a simple shift in awareness.

Once you're in the midst of a lucid dream, of course, you won't want to just sit back and watch. So in addition, Week Two tells you how to traverse the dream terrain through flight, how to conjure dream images through whirling, and how to sustain the lucid state by staring at your hands, or the sky.

You will also apply the incubation techniques you learned in Week One to the lucid dream. By focusing on appropriate words and symbols before you fall asleep, you can conjure dream characters from Princess Di to your deceased Aunt Millie to Attila the Hun.

Perhaps most important, you will learn the art of *dream weaving*—consciously altering the details in your dream. After you have mastered Week Two exercises, you should be able to convert your dream roses to daisies, and your dream bathtub to the starship *Enterprise,* complete with Captain Kirk. As you practice the dream weaving exercise, you may become adept at creating entire lucid dream scenarios, including great adventures, passionate love scenes, or even a dream detective series that continues from night to night.

One word of advice: the most advanced lucid dreamers do not necessarily alter their dreams just to watch the seasons change or the walls cave in. In fact, more often, they use dream flying, dream whirling, and dream weaving skills to further explore their dream landscape—to climb that dream mountain, or open that dream safe, so they can gain further insights into the unconscious universe beyond and within.

Finally, do not feel upset if you don't start having lucid dreams on the first day of Week Two. Give yourself time, and relax. Putting pressure on yourself can only slow the delicate inner mechanism so crucial to lucid dreaming. Remember, everyone is different. If you diligently practice Week Two exercises and allow yourself to enjoy the process, your lucid-dream experiences should begin soon.

DAY 8

REALITY CHECK

A lucid dream is one in which you are consciously aware of the fact that you are dreaming. As we've already discussed, becoming aware of your thoughts while you're asleep and dreaming can be helped along by becoming more consciously aware of your thoughts while you're wide awake. One way to achieve this generally increased state of awareness is to regularly ask yourself if you're awake or dreaming as you go about your everyday activities. This approach, often suggested by dream researchers, is a natural extension of the dream rehearsal exercise you practiced on Day 6. By conducting regular "reality checks," asking yourself if you might be dreaming, you should eventually find yourself posing the question while in the midst of a dream.

Begin Day 8 much as you normally would, eating breakfast and conducting errands or going to work. But every half hour or so, stop, look around you, and simply ask yourself, *Is this a dream?* Let's say you're taking the subway from your apartment to your downtown firm. First study the people around you. Do they have normal, everyday faces? Or does that dour businessman to your left boast a third eye blinking in the middle of his forehead? What about the colorfully painted billboard to your right? Look at the images displayed on it once, then look at them again. Were the images different each time you saw them, or the same? If they differed from one moment to the next, and you're not looking at some newfangled high-tech billboard, you must be dreaming.

As you enter your office, study the details there too. Does the view outside your window include the same familiar scenery, or are you surprised to see a moat filled with alligators, Oz, or Tranquility Base on the Moon? If the scene outside your window is dramatically askew, you can bet you're in a dream.

One of the best ways to check whether or not you're dreaming is to deliberately try to change some aspect of your immediate surroundings through thought alone. For example, let's say you're seated in a restaurant and the waiter brings you four meatballs for lunch. Before you take a bite, look at the plate and mentally will the four meatballs into eight. If the transformation takes place, you are most certainly in a dream. Continue to ask yourself, *Is this a dream?* throughout the rest of the day. Then answer your question with an appropriate reality check.

Remember, you can usually recognize a dream through the occurrence of anything weirdly inappropriate or bizarre— particularly if you can bring about such occurrences through deliberate thought. For instance, if you are flying on your own, if you are breathing underwater or in outer space without special equipment, if you find yourself lifting a Mack truck with your bare hands, or making wild, passionate love to a purple gnome, you are most likely having a dream. If your feelings and thoughts seem oddly inconsistent, or if the structure of reality is constantly shifting, you are probably dreaming.

If your frequent reality checks suggest that you're not presently in a dream, remind yourself that you are instead awake and conscious of everything going on around you. Every time you realize that you are awake, say to yourself, *This is not a dream*. Then focus on the sensations and perceptions of waking consciousness. If you *do* feel you're in the midst of a dream, on the other hand, say to yourself, *I am dreaming*.

Before you go to bed, tell yourself, *Tonight I will recognize that I am dreaming while in the midst of a dream*. Write this sentence in your dream journal. Then place the journal beside your bed and repeat the sentence again as you drift off to sleep. Most important, remember to perform the same reality checks in your lucid dreams that you conducted during the day. If you should awaken after a dream in the middle of the night, stop to consider what was dreamlike about it. Then repeat the thought, *Tonight I will recognize that I am dreaming while in the midst of a dream*, and allow yourself to fall back to sleep.

> **Dream Alert**—For the next three weeks of the Creative Sleep Program, remember to conduct reality checks on a regular basis throughout your waking day. Each night before you go to bed and just as you're drifting off to sleep, quietly give yourself permission to have lucid dreams and to remember your dream experiences upon awakening. It is also important that you conduct reality checks while you're dreaming; this approach will help you recognize that you are having a dream. Remember to record your dreams in your dream journal as soon as possible after you awaken in the morning.

DAY 9

I LOVE LUCIDITY

On Day 9 we tap a technique recommended by psychologist Stephen LaBerge of the Stanford University Sleep Research Center. Using this method, you will learn to recognize the semiconscious state most everyone enters after waking from a dream. You will then learn to convert this semiconscious state into a lucid dream.

We suggest that you begin Day 9 much as you began Day

8. On a regular basis throughout the day, continue to ask yourself whether or not you are dreaming. Before you go to bed, write in your dream journal, *Tonight I will recognize that I am dreaming while in the midst of a dream,* and repeat this phrase to yourself as you drift off to sleep.

During the early morning hours you are likely to awaken spontaneously from a nonlucid dream. When you do, lie quietly in bed without moving or opening your eyes and think about the dream you've just had. Review the dream in your mind in as much detail as possible, absorbing the emotional impact of the setting, characters, plot, and overall aesthetic imagery. Review the dream several times in your thoughts, until you've more or less committed it to conscious memory.

Then review the dream again, this time adding one element that was clearly missing before: as you replay the dream in your thoughts, approach it as if you, the dreamer, are conscious of the dream as it is happening. Repeat the phrase *I will recognize a dream when I'm dreaming* and allow yourself to drift off to sleep.

If you follow these instructions, you will probably find yourself falling backward from your nearly conscious state into the realm of sleep and dreams. You may possibly find yourself replaying the dream you just left, or generating a whole new dream that may or may not include elements of your previous dream. In either case, you may soon find yourself in the midst of a full-blown lucid dream.

> **Dream Alert**—If you think you may be having a lucid dream, remember to conduct a reality check using the approach described on Day 8. Also remember to record all lucid and nonlucid dreams in your dream journal.

DAY 10

DREAMER'S
GUIDE TO THE
UNIVERSE

One of the best ways to consciously influence the general plot and setting of a lucid dream is through straightforward dream incubation. On Day 10, therefore, you will apply the art of incubation to the lucid dream.

First, make certain that your external dream environment reflects your primary intention: to become conscious in your dreams. To signal this intention to your unconscious mind, we suggest that you select what we call a *lucidity symbol* and place it in the room where you sleep. This lucidity symbol may be a picture of the universe, an attractive Tiffany-style lamp, a rubber eyeball from a novelty catalogue, or anything else that will serve as a personal symbolic reminder of your intention to have a lucid dream. Remember, the symbol is not intended to induce a *particular* dream, but rather to serve as a reminder of your general goal.

After you've selected a lucidity symbol and placed it in your sleep environment, go about the normal activities of your day. As you did on Days 8 and 9, continue performing frequent reality checks and reaffirming your intention to have a lucid dream.

As the hours pass, you should also decide upon a destination for tonight's dream: your old hometown during the fifties; Hong Kong, circa 3089; or even Sydney, Australia in prehistoric times. Whatever locale and time period you choose, you should subtly contemplate the intended focus on your upcoming dream throughout the day. Be specific. The more precisely you express your intended dream destination in your thoughts, the more likely you are to actually experience being there at night in your dreams.

Later, about an hour before you plan to go to bed, surround your lucidity symbol with potent incubation images that remind you of your intended dream. If you want to dream about the Civil War, for instance, you might dig up a picture of Abraham Lincoln or a tiny Confederate flag. If you'd like to spend the night with Gumby, you might place a container of Play-Doh and a toy Gumby figure next to your lucidity symbol. Arrange all your incubation objects or images in an aesthetically interesting fashion, even placing one or more of these objects in bed with you, if you wish. You may also enhance the atmosphere by burning incense or playing music that you feel will be particularly conducive to your desired lucid-dream experience.

Right before you finally turn off the light and go to sleep, sit beside the "lucid-dream altar" you've created, and articulate in your mind once more the desired destination of your intended lucid dream. Then, using your special pen, describe your destination in a single phrase in your dream journal. Be as precise as possible. If you wish to experience the Civil War, for example, write, *Tonight I will return to the days of Abraham Lincoln;* you might even draw a picture of his famous top hat.

You must also remember to focus upon your intention to become lucid in this dream. Therefore, follow the first phrase in your journal with a second, such as, *The next time I dream about the Civil War, I will recognize that I am dreaming.* As soon as you've done this, turn off the light and go to sleep.

Continue focusing on your intended destination and your desire to have a lucid dream as you drift off more and more deeply into sleep. Picture in your mind the incubation objects you've placed around you in the room. Quietly remind yourself of your intention to dream about the subject at hand. Also remind yourself that you will remember the details of all related dreams when you wake up.

As an alternative to inducing a "theme dream," lucid dreamers may use dream incubation to help solve personal or creative problems. If you're still wondering about how to deal with your boyfriend, Melvin, for instance, casually focus your thoughts on him throughout the day. Put a picture of him next to your lucidity symbol. And at night, before you go to bed, write in your dream journal, *What should I do with Melvin?*

or, *Do I really love Melvin at all?* Tell yourself to gain some insight into your relationship as you dream, and to be aware of the experience as you're dreaming. Later, if you realize that you're in a dream, you may even consciously seek out Melvin to talk things over.

On the other hand, if you feel stumped by some issue in cosmology, think about black holes, superstrings, and the curvature of space. Post a picture of the Milky Way in your dream environment when you get home, and before you go to bed at night, formulate an appropriate goal. For instance, you might determine to visit the far side of Neptune in a lucid dream. Then describe your intention as clearly as possible in your dream journal: *Tonight I'll visit Neptune and I'll know that I'm dreaming.* If you do conjure Neptune in a lucid dream, you might then decide to look around for physicist Stephen W. Hawking relaxing under the stars. You might ask him for the location of the missing mass of the universe, or the secret to unifying the four forces of nature into one.

Feel free to be innovative as you adapt the lucid-dream incubation technique to best serve your personal, creative, or intellectual needs. Rather than merely incubating a general dream setting, for instance, you might invite specific characters into your dreams. You can even seek out dream guides who have died. For instance, Ernest Hemingway might tell you how to overcome your writer's block, giving you an idea for a blockbuster novel in the process.

We recommend that you take the lucid-dream incubation process slowly and realistically. Now that you have studied the basic technique, you can allow each small successful experience to help you build confidence in your creative dreaming abilities before you add additional dimensions of complexity. The less pressure you put on yourself and the more relaxed you are with the process, the more likely you will be to experience your desired dreams.

Dream Alert—If you awaken from a dream at any point during the night, practice inducing lucidity by mentally falling backward into your desired dream. If you find yourself having a lucid dream about any subject, remember to conduct a reality check using the techniques you practiced on Day 8. Also, remember to record your dreams in your dream journal as soon as possible after awakening. At least for the duration of the Creative Sleep Program, leave your lucidity symbol in a selected spot within your sleep environment. Whenever you happen to notice this symbol in passing, subtly reaffirm your intention to have lucid dreams.

DAY 11

WHO'S FLYING NOW?

Have you ever wanted to fly like Superman, soaring across the continents or through the vastness of space with no more effort than walking down the block? Would you like to visit the Louvre in Paris or the Incan ruins, yet be back home in time for the Super Bowl? Do you want to explore Antarctica without even getting cold? If so, then dream flying may be for you.

Dream flying can be one of the most truly enjoyable, even ecstatic, lucid-dream experiences you're ever likely to have. The sensation of flying in your dreams can be as exhilarating as a ride on the Cyclone or as calming as a week of sunsets at the beach. It may even save your "life" during that all-time favorite dream terror, the endless fall. What's more, once you learn how to fly in your lucid dreams, you'll have acquired a mode of dream transportation that can take you virtually anywhere in the magic kingdom of dream reality—even back and forth in time.

To fly in your dreams, it is helpful to learn an advanced version of the dream incubation technique you practiced on Day 10. As before, make sure your personal dream sanctuary reflects your intention—in this case, to fly in your lucid dreams. To begin, look at your lucidity symbol. Remove all other images and objects from its immediate vicinity and replace them with pictures of birds, planes, or even Superman in flight.

Then leave the house and go about your day. As you have on previous days, continue to conduct reality checks and reaffirm your desire to have a lucid dream. Also spend a good part of the day thinking about how much you would like to fly in your dreams. We also suggest that as you walk around your waking world you look up at the sky and observe the flight of birds and planes. If you have time, you might even visit an airport or aviary, or watch a few episodes of the old "Superman" television series starring George Reeves. (We recommend these as opposed to the more recent film series starring Christopher Reeve simply because the original version included more flying.) The more you think about the process of flying, the more likely you are to fly in your dreams, and to be lucid at the time.

After you arrive home from your day's activities, recall any flying dreams you had in the past, and decide upon a dream destination. Coin a key dream flight phrase and keep repeating it. For instance, you might say, *I want to fly*, or, *Tonight I fly*, or, *Tonight I will fly to Papua, New Guinea*.

Before you go to bed, spend some time relaxing in your dream environment and calmly noticing your lucidity symbol and the incubation images of flight you've chosen for your dream altar. Then, using your special pen, write your dream incubation phrase, describing your desire to fly in your dream journal. If you have a specific destination in mind, go ahead and mention that as well. A simple single sentence modeled on the ones above should work best.

Now put down your dream journal and turn off the light. As you drift off to sleep, silently repeat the sentence you've just written. Continue focusing on your intention to fly and to be lucid in your dreams. Also focus on your intended dream destination. Picture the images of flight that you've placed around you in the room. Imagine a feeling of weightlessness, or envision yourself soaring like a glider; tap the flight images that feel most comfortable for you. Quietly give yourself permission to dream about the subject at hand and to be consciously aware of dreaming. Also remind yourself that you will remember all related dreams when you wake up.

Dream Alert—If you awaken from a dream at any point during the night, use the approach of falling back into a dream to help stimulate lucid-dream flight. After you wake up spontaneously from a dream, lie in bed quietly, neither moving nor opening your eyes, and think about the dream you've just had. Sustaining a state of semiconsciousness, rehearse the details of the flying dream you would like to experience, and while you're falling back to sleep, say in your thoughts, *Tonight, I'll fly.* Imagine yourself flying to your chosen destination in your dream as you fall more and more deeply asleep. Even if you don't immediately experience full-blown lucid-dream flight the first time you practice this exercise, chances are that you will, before too long.

Dream Alert—As always, you should conduct reality checks whenever you believe you might be having a lucid dream. If you find yourself flying without mechanical assistance, you'll have pretty convincing evidence that you're dreaming. If you realize that you're dreaming but haven't yet experienced dream flight, use the opportunity to remind yourself to fly. Throw your arms over your head and leap into the air like Superman, flap your outstretched arms like giant wings, or just focus your thoughts so intensely on the idea of flying that you cannot help but create the experience of flight in your dream. Using these methods, you will then very likely take off.

Dream Alert—As you become more proficient at dream flight, you should be able to perform increasingly intricate maneuvers in your lucid dreams. For instance, you might begin your dream flight efforts by simply floating a short distance above the ground. You might then be able to glide astronautlike through the air for several feet at a time. With practice, you should eventually be able to increase your navigational ability, your altitude, and your speed. You might send yourself on dream flights to Europe, Mars, and galaxies beyond our own.

Dream Alert—Remember to record all dreams, including any flying dreams, in your dream journal.

DAY 12

WHIRL WITHOUT
END

Even after you've induced a desired lucid dream, it is easy to wake up or drift right back into ordinary dream sleep. What's more, even if you do sustain your lucid dream, you may still have trouble controlling the activities taking place within the dream itself.

Dream researchers such as Stanford's LaBerge have found that deliberately spinning your dream body like a top can extend the duration of your lucid dreams. Spinning may also enable you to influence the setting of your dream and can serve as a means of travel much like dream flight.

You can learn the technique of dream spinning in much the same way you learned to achieve dream flight. First, as you go about Day 12, continue to ask yourself if you are dreaming, and continue to assert your desire to have lucid dreams. Then, sometime during the evening before you go to bed, choose a lucid-dream destination.

This time, don't just choose something general, like New York City or the state of Idaho. Choose a highly specific destination instead, like a front row seat at the Metropolitan Opera House for a performance of *La Traviata,* or the student center building of the bucolic college campus at Pocatello. Though it may be more difficult to achieve, you might even choose a destination in the distant past or future, vowing to chat with Plato or visit a space colony near Pluto in the year 3000 A.D.

Once you have chosen your destination, gather some objects or images that bring it to mind and put these near the lucidity symbol you keep in your dream room. (Remove the objects you have used to incubate other dreams on previous nights.) As clearly and precisely as possible, record your intended destination in your dream journal, along with a phrase signifying your intention to have a lucid dream. Then shut off the light and go to bed.

To reach your lucid-dream goal, first envision your specific destination and silently reaffirm your desire to have a lucid dream as you fall asleep. Let the objects that symbolize your goal pass through your mind.

Once asleep, you may find yourself in the midst of a lucid dream. If you have not reached your intended dream destination, however, just spin your dream body like a pirouetting dancer or a top. Whirl faster and faster, until your present surroundings seem to blur, and your desired surroundings begin coming into focus. Use the same technique if you sense yourself waking up, or if you sense that your lucidity is starting to fade. Spin fast enough, and your immersion in the lucid-dream state should be sustained. If you *do* wake up, however, don't be concerned; mastering the dream whirling technique can take practice.

While many researchers recommend spinning as the preferred means of sustaining a lucid dream, we believe that many other techniques can work just as well. For instance, writer Carlos Castaneda suggests that the lucid-dream state may be sustained simply by looking at your hands in a dream. As far as Castaneda is concerned, if you decide to look at your hands before falling asleep, then actually look at your hands in your dream, you should be able to sustain the lucid state, at least until the image of your hands somehow fades.

We suspect that it doesn't much matter whether you are whirling, looking at your hands, or doing something else altogether. You may decide to hop like a kangaroo if this works for you, or simply to look up at the sky and tell yourself, *Things are looking up*. If you commit to completing a particular action before your dream and actually follow through while the dream is in progress and perform the action you've planned, your dream images should remain sharp and the lucid-dream state should be sustained. In all likelihood, the degree of your conscious intention to sustain a lucid dream is the deciding factor in your ability to maintain this state.

Dream Alert—As always, remember to practice dream recollection techniques and to record your dreams in your dream journal as soon as possible after waking up in the morning.

DAY 13

DREAM
WEAVING

During the past few days you have learned to induce and sustain lucid dreams, and to consciously navigate your dream terrain. On Day 13 we will begin to teach you yet another level of conscious dream control: the ability to deliberately will the alteration of dream characters, scenery, props, and plot. By practicing Day 13 techniques throughout the rest of the Creative Sleep Program, you should eventually learn to direct your dream experiences as skillfully as Steven Spielberg directed *E.T.*

Begin Day 13 much like the other days of Week Two, by checking reality and quietly affirming to yourself your willingness to have a lucid dream. However, as you go about your day, also keep another thought in mind: that like Merlin the Magician or Glinda, the Good Witch of the North, you will claim the power to create, destroy, or alter objects and characters in your dreams.

Indeed, we suggest that as you go about your day you imagine yourself in the persona of a film director with access to scenery, props, a cast of thousands, and the best special effects technology in the world. During the early part of the day think of a recent movie that disappointed you, and redirect the action in your mind. How would the film turn out if the changes you envision could really be made? Now consider the sequencing of a film that you, as a director, might create from scratch. What would the film be about? Who would star in it? Where would it take place?

After you have carried out the exercise described above, choose some quiet part of your day—your lunch hour, perhaps—to visit a populated area where you can simply sit and look around without being disturbed. An outdoor café, a shopping mall, or even a large bowling alley would work well for this part of the exercise. Sit down and focus your attention

on the activities taking place around you. Notice your surroundings, from the plastic vegetation to the store facades to
the signs. Notice the people inhabiting your environment. Pay
attention to any odors or sounds drifting your way. For instance, is that exotic-looking couple at the next table in the
middle of a fight? Is the woman's scent Jean Naté? Does that
man behind the counter seem extremely happy, or unduly
upset? That heavyset woman with the oversize bowling ball
bag—is she a retired trucker, or a housewife coming from an
exercise class? Where did she get that raspy, asthmatic cough?
What's really in the bag?

Spend about fifteen minutes consciously observing your
environment. Then imagine that the people and props, the
music and the aromas all around you, are elements of a new
type of entertainment—a "multisensory" film—of which you
have complete creative control. Imagine that you are the
director, sent to pull this project together.

Let's say you're at an outdoor café, seated near the exotic
couple embroiled in a fight. Study their food and their clothes,
their wrinkles and their facial features, and in your mind's eye,
begin to imagine change. Stare at the woman's greasy ham-
burger until, at least to you, she's eating steak tartare. Do you
find the Jean Naté unpleasant? Focus on your sense of smell
until, at least to your nostrils, the perfume is Givenchy. The
gentlemen has dark receding hair, but you can change him into
a long-haired blond. The café itself is okay for a lunch-hour
sandwich, perhaps, but if you focus enough, you can "place"
it on the Left Bank of Paris and imagine yourself having some
French onion soup. Using this technique, imagine yourself
changing detail after detail of the surrounding scenario, until
your aesthetic sensibility is satisfied.

Now imagine taking your real-life "film" even further by
creating a screenplay for your couple to act out. "See" the
man storming off, going to the airport, and getting on a plane.
Envision the woman overturning the table, white linen cloth,
rose, and all, and tyrannizing the patrons with a gun. Whatever
the scenario, follow it through to its most surrealistic and
captivating conclusion in your mind. Don't forget to alter plot
line and other details whenever you feel the story has lost its
creative thrust.

When you feel satisfied with your imagined experience in this exercise, continue with the rest of your day, finally returning home. Enter your dream environment, and before you retire to bed, see in your mind the "film" you created during your quiet period earlier in the day. Focus especially on the small details you changed during the earliest moments. Then, using your special pen, write in your dream journal, *Tonight I will alter my dreams*. Shut off the light and review this afternoon's thought exercises as you drift more and more deeply into sleep.

Remember, start slowly. The first time you try to influence the images in your lucid dreams, just tackle a few things; turn that apple tree into an orange tree, for instance, or turn your walk-in closet into an Old West saloon. Later, as you perfect the dream weaving technique, you should be able to alter virtually anything in your dreams, invoking entire cavalries, or a rain of frogs. If you don't feel like flying to your intended destination in your dream, you should even be able to bring your dream destination directly to you. (You can learn to do this through an advanced version of the dream weaving exercise presented in Week Three.) Eventually, you should be able to combine dream weaving with additional skills such as dream spinning and dream flying to create exciting, extraordinary, and highly creative customized dream experiences. You may even use the technique you first practiced in today's exercise to explore alternative solutions to a number of personal questions and intellectual or creative dilemmas.

Dream Alert—For particularly powerful control over the details of your dreams, you can apply dream weaving techniques after spontaneously awakening from a dream during the early morning hours and then falling back into a lucid dream.

Dream Alert—Please remember, altering the details of a lucid dream can often wake you up, bringing that particular dream to an end. If this happens to you, just sustain a state of semiconsciousness as you continue the dream weaving exercise in your imagination. This will enable you to experience the symbolic impact of the exercise without feeling that you have in any way failed.

Dream Alert—Remember to practice dream recollection, and to record all remembered dreams in your dream journal. From now on, note all the dream elements you have managed to alter using the dream weaving technique.

DAY 14

FREE DREAMING

By now, you've probably come a long way toward tapping the potential of lucid dreams for personal growth. Whether you've sought creative solutions to professional problems or guidance in your love life, you have probably discovered that lucid dreaming can enable you to access the mother lode of knowledge normally buried in the outback of your unconscious mind.

On Day 14 of the Creative Sleep Program, we recommend a night of *free dreaming*—that is, dreaming without either deliberately influencing the content of your dreams or consciously inducing lucidity. Doing so can give your unconscious mind an opportunity to blow off a little residual psychological steam and balance out some of the more consciously structured dreaming experiences of the past two weeks.

In all likelihood you will find yourself spontaneously entering a lucid-dream state at some point during the night. Use the opportunity to passively observe your dreams and assess any subjective changes that may have taken place in the quality and intensity of your dreams over the past two weeks.

Dream Alert—As usual, record your dreams in your dream journal when you first wake up in the morning.

Congratulations! You have just completed Week Two of the Creative Sleep Program.

WEEK TWO LUCID DREAMING

DAY 8 REALITY CHECK	**DAY 9** I LOVE LUCIDITY	**DAY 10** DREAMER'S GUIDE TO THE UNIVERSE	
In the morning, recall and record your dreams. Throughout the day, stop and ask yourself whether or not you are dreaming. Before you drift off to sleep, vow to recognize a dream while you are in the midst of it.	In the morning, recall and record your dreams. Throughout the day, stop and ask yourself whether or not you are dreaming. Before you drift off to sleep, vow to recognize a dream while you are in the midst of it. If you wake up from a nonlucid dream in the early morning hours, review the details, vowing once more to recognize a dream while you are dreaming. Drift back off to sleep.	In the morning, recall and record your dreams. Throughout the day, stop and ask yourself whether or not you are dreaming. Select a lucid-dream symbol and place it in your sleep environment. Select a destination for tonight's dream. Surround your lucidity symbol with incubation images of your intended dream destination. Write your goal in your dream journal.	Before you drift off to sleep, think about your intended dream destination and vow to have a lucid dream.

DAY 11 WHO'S FLYING NOW?		DAY 12 WHIRL WITHOUT END	
In the morning, recall and record your dreams. Throughout the day, stop and ask yourself whether or not you are dreaming. Assert your desire to have lucid dreams. Surround your lucidity symbol with images of flight. During the day, focus on birds and airplanes. Tell yourself that tonight you will fly in your dreams.	Before you go to bed, choose a dream destination and vow to fly there. Write your goal in your dream journal. Repeat your dream goal to yourself as you drift off to sleep.	In the morning, recall and record your dreams. Throughout the day, stop and ask yourself whether or not you are dreaming. Throughout the day, assert your desire to have lucid dreams. Choose a dream destination. Choose objects to symbolize this destination and place them near your lucidity symbol.	Record your intended dream destination and your intention to have a lucid dream in your journal before going to bed. Drift off to sleep. Once you find yourself in a lucid dream, spin your dream body until the desired dream destination comes into focus. If you start to wake up, whirl your dream body faster and faster, until you feel that the lucid dream state has been sustained.

(continued)

WEEK TWO   LUCID DREAMING (continued)

DAY 13 DREAM WEAVING		**DAY 14** FREE DREAMING
In the morning, recall and record your dreams. Throughout the day, stop and ask yourself whether or not you are dreaming. Throughout the day, assert your desire to have lucid dreams. Throughout the day, tell yourself that you will be able to create, destroy, or alter objects in your dreams. Sometime during the day find a quiet place to sit. Then imagine yourself altering the scene around you.	In the morning, recall and record your dreams. Go about your day much as you did before you started the Creative Sleep Program. Go to bed without doing anything special at all.	Before you go to bed, remember the scene you imagined altering earlier. Write about your intention to alter you dreams in your dream journal. Recall the scene you "altered" earlier in the day as you drift off to sleep. Once you find yourself in a lucid dream, remember to alter at least one or two dream details.

WEEK THREE

HIGH LUCIDITY

WEEK
THREE

•

H I G H   L U C I D I T Y

*T*he Dream Yogis of ancient Tibet were known for an extraordinary mental feat. Using an extremely potent method of guided imagery, they are said to have retreated more and more deeply inside themselves until they started to dream—without ever losing conscious awareness.

According to *Tibetan Yoga and Secret Doctrines,* edited by Oxford scholar W. Y. Evans-Wentz, the Dream Yogis had almost total control over broad aspects of their highly lucid dreams. Using their lucid dreaming abilities, the Yogis were able to create endless dream Edens, explore alternate realities, and come to terms with such issues as the nature of reality and the meaning of life.

In the latter part of the twentieth century, the Dream Yogis' exact methodology remains obscure. In Week Three of the Creative Sleep Program, however, we present high lucidity, *our* version of the Tibetan Yogis' "conscious dreams."

In line with our own research, high lucidity is based on a technique known as *alert relaxation,* in which the body becomes increasingly relaxed while the mind remains alert. Athletes often enter this altered state of consciousness to mentally rehearse their maneuvers. In our other book, *Have an Out-of-Body Experience in 30 Days: The Free Flight Program* (also available from St. Martin's Press), we show readers how to use alert relaxation to experience the expansive feeling of separation between body and mind.

In the Creative Sleep Program you will learn how to use alert relaxation to intensify your spontaneous mental imagery until it evolves into a conscious dream. Since you maintain conscious awareness through the entire experience, high lucidity should provide you with a greater degree of influence over your dreams. Once you have become experienced in this technique, you should find your lucid dreams far more vivid and intense—and far more malleable—than before. In the altered state of high lucidity, you can learn to change dream weather, alter dream scenery, and gain increasing insight into the range of imaginary entities inhabiting your dreams. Of course, achieving high lucidity takes practice, but it is not as difficult as you might believe. In many ways it is similar to the experience of returning to a lucid dream state after just awakening, a technique you've already learned in Week Two.

Even if you are not immediately successful at achieving high lucidity, we recommend that once you learn the basic technique on Days 15, 16, and 17, you continue practicing it on a nightly basis, at least throughout the next two weeks of the Creative Sleep Program. By doing so, we have every expectation that you will eventually learn to enter the intense state of high lucidity directly from waking consciousness, claiming increasingly more power over your dreams.

DAY 15

ALTERED STATES

On Day 15 you will learn the technique of *alert relaxation,* in which the body enters a state of deep relaxation while the mind remains acutely alert. While in the altered state of alert relaxation, you will remain mentally alert while slowly becoming so relaxed that you fall asleep. Through this process you should be able to enter a lucid dream directly from the waking state, without ever losing conscious awareness as you're falling asleep.

By entering your lucid dreams in this way, you will achieve a state we call *high lucidity,* the focus of Week Three. High lucidity will enable you to intensify your lucid dreams, giving you considerably more control over the images and actions within.

> **Dream Alert**—Read the rest of the instructions for Day 15 in advance, so that you can carry out the necessary preparations and be ready to practice the entire exercise without interruption.

To experience the greatest potential benefit from these instructions, we ask that, at least initially, you have a friend or partner guide you through the relaxation exercise that follows. Begin by finding a private and comfortable place to lie down. Then have your friend slowly and quietly read the instructions aloud step by step, exactly as they're written below, pausing briefly where indicated. You may also wish to make a tape recording of you or your friend reading these instructions so that you can practice on your own after this initial session:

> Take a deep breath, let it out slowly, stretch your muscles, and relax. Now imagine that warm currents of mental energy are very slowly moving up through the soles of your feet toward your ankles.
>
> Feel the muscles in your feet gradually warming and relaxing as you imagine the currents passing through them. [Pause.] Imagine that the currents continue moving up through your calves [pause], into your thighs [pause], through your hips [pause] and buttocks [pause] and into your lower back and abdomen. [Pause.] Proceed very slowly, giving yourself time for each group of muscles to become fully relaxed before allowing the imaginary currents to move on to the next area of your body. [Pause.] Feel the muscles in your legs becoming heavy, warm, and relaxed and sinking down into the chair beneath you. [Pause.]
>
> When you feel your legs becoming deeply relaxed, imagine the currents moving in a clockwise motion around your abdomen [pause], up along your spine [pause], and through the front of your torso into your chest [pause] and shoulders. Feel the muscles in your stomach and lower back releasing any tightness or tension as the current passes through them. [Pause.] Allow a feeling of general well-being to begin flowing through your body along with the imaginary currents as you continue to relax. [Pause.]

When the lower half of your body feels relaxed [pause], imagine the currents flowing upward through your ribs and shoulders [pause], warming and relaxing the upper part of your body [pause] and leaving your back and chest feeling completely warm and free of any stress or tension. [Pause.] Imagine the currents turning around to move downward through your arms and toward your fingertips [pause]; imagine the currents swirling around through your fingers and hands and then moving upward once more [pause], back through your arms and neck [pause] toward the top of your head. [Pause.]

Now feel the muscles in your neck and face gradually becoming warm and relaxed as the imaginary currents pass through them. [Pause.] Then imagine the currents flowing out through the top of your head [pause], leaving your entire body feeling comfortably warm [pause], heavy [pause], and relaxed. [Pause.] Feel your body sinking down into the chair beneath you.

Once you gain experience, you should be able to enter the state of alert relaxation more and more quickly, without needing anyone to read the instructions to you. For Day 15, however, it is sufficient simply to practice becoming deeply relaxed while maintaining a state of mental alertness, taking as much time and using as much assistance as you need to comfortably achieve this state.

Once you have entered the state of alert relaxation, maintain it for twenty or thirty minutes before gradually bringing yourself back to full waking consciousness. You may accomplish this simply by wiggling your fingers and toes, concentrating on your immediate surroundings, and opening your eyes.

Dream Alert—Read the instructions for Day 16 before going to bed so that you may make the necessary advance preparations. As you're falling asleep at night, once again practice the alert relaxation exercise you learned earlier in the day. While in this state of alert relaxation, quietly affirm your desire to have a lucid dream. If you should find yourself in the midst of a lucid dream, practice the dream weaving techniques you learned in Week Two. Tomorrow morning, after you recall your dreams, record the results in your dream journal.

DAY 16

THE ADVENTURES
OF GUMBY

On Day 16 you will move a step closer to achieving the state of high lucidity. Today's session should be conducted at least three hours before you normally go to sleep. This will make you less likely to just drift off into unconscious sleep while following the instructions. Begin by selecting a private room where you can lie down and relax without being disturbed, and where you can eventually go to sleep. The room should be one in which you can play a television set at low volume. It would be ideal if the television were connected to a video cassette recorder (VCR), though this is not absolutely essential.

What is essential is that the television or VCR be set up to play a cartoon show or nature feature for at least an hour. As far as your choice of program material, public television nature programs would work well for this exercise, because they are broadcast without commercial interruptions. We especially recommend, however, playing a video of a cartoon or other animated feature rich in the kind of surrealistic imagery often found in dreams. Our own favorite choice for this exercise would be any adventure featuring the beloved clay character Gumby.

The Gumby character exists in a completely surrealistic and flexible reality that often succeeds in capturing the quality of dreams. Gumby, the master of this reality, also possesses the kind of creative imagination it takes to respond affirmatively, effectively, and with good humor to his dreamlike experiences. Other appropriate cartoons include the *Real Ghostbusters, Muppet Babies, The Smurfs,* and *Fantasia.* We also recommend *Pee-wee's Playhouse.*

Once you have selected an appropriate video or program for this exercise, turn down the lights and turn on the television at a low but clearly audible volume. It would also be helpful to turn down the brightness control on your set as much as possible without obliterating the picture. Find a comfortable place where you can lie down to watch without straining your neck. Get cozy and enjoy the show for at least half an hour. Imagine yourself existing in the reality of the characters you're observing, and allow yourself to absorb the images as fully as possible.

After roughly thirty minutes have passed, roll over onto your back, close your eyes, and continue listening to the sound track in the background. Allow your imagination to fill in the pictures to go along with the sounds you're hearing. As you do this, take a deep breath, stretch your muscles, and relax. While continuing to focus on the background sounds and any images they help to generate in your mind, imagine warm currents of mental energy very slowly moving up through the soles of your feet toward your ankles. Then enter a state of alert relaxation as you did on Day 15, adding the additional focus, described below:

As you become more and more deeply relaxed, allow your thoughts to drift off into the mental images generated by the television show or video you've been watching; these images may be generated by memories of the show *and* by the sounds continuing to play in the background. Before long, you'll probably find these images taking on a kind of spontaneous life of their own, having less to do with the external sounds in the room than with your own evolving internal experience. Don't try to force this process; rather, allow it to emerge on its own. As much as possible, consciously observe your internal images without losing awareness. You can accomplish this by deliberately directing your attention back toward the sounds coming from the television set whenever you notice yourself beginning to lose consciousness. As you do this, tell yourself that you are consciously alert and observing the impact that these sounds have on your thoughts.

For now, you should not be trying to fall asleep while practicing this exercise. Rather, you should attempt to sustain a deep state of alert relaxation. If you should find yourself accidentally losing conscious awareness while practicing this exercise, however, don't worry about it. The moment you feel yourself returning to consciousness, continue the exercise from wherever you left off.

After thirty or forty-five minutes, complete the exercise by gradually focusing more and more of your attention on the sound of the television in the background, and on your physical presence in your immediate surroundings.

Just before you are ready to go to bed, spend some time quietly watching the same type of television program you used for the first part of this exercise. When you're ready to go to sleep, again enter a state of alert relaxation, this time with the television turned off. While in this state of alert relaxation, quietly affirm your desire to have a lucid dream, then fall asleep.

> **Dream Alert**—If you should find yourself in the midst of a lucid dream, practice the dream weaving techniques you learned in Week Two. Tomorrow morning, after you recall your dreams, record the results in your dream journal.

DAY 17

HIGH LUCIDITY

On Day 17 you will learn how to enter the dream state of high lucidity. Again, by *high lucidity,* we mean the state of acute dream lucidity that results when you carry your conscious awareness directly into a dream.

To achieve high lucidity, you must take the exercises of the past two days one step further. Your goal: to generate what's known as *hypnagogic imagery,* vivid but conscious mental pictures that emerge as you hover between wakefulness and sleep. By following our instructions, you should be able to generate hypnagogic images and follow them into bona fide lucid dreams without ever losing conscious awareness. The result: high lucidity, in which you should have even more control over your lucid dreams than you did before.

Begin today's session an hour before you would normally go to bed. This will enable you to carry out the exercise completely and then follow it directly into your full night's sleep. As before, practice in a private room where you can relax and then sleep without being disturbed. Again, arrange to watch an appropriate television program or video, at low volume and brightness, for at least an hour. Please make sure that the episodes you watch today are different from those you viewed the day before. We also recommend that, if at all possible, you arrange to have your television turned off after you have fallen asleep. If you are using a video recorder, it should simply turn itself off automatically at the end of the tape. If you are watching a television without a VCR, you might hook your set to a separate timer so that it will automatically disconnect. Or, alternatively, you can ask someone to quietly slip in and turn off the television at a prearranged time.

After you have made the arrangements, lie back and absorb the images you've selected. After about thirty minutes, roll over onto your back and close your eyes. Continue listening to the program playing in the background while filling in the pictures with your own mental images. As you do this, gradually enter a state of alert relaxation.

As you become increasingly relaxed, focus on the images in your mind while also doing your best to maintain conscious awareness. Allow the images to become as spontaneous as possible, using the audio input from the television to help generate fresh images as the earlier ones fade. As much as possible, allow all of these images to blend and interact with one another, and to take on a life of their own. As the exercise continues, these images should become increasingly spontaneous, or hypnagogic, in nature. Whenever you feel yourself losing conscious awareness, focus your attention more intensely on the sound of the television, and say to yourself, *I'm entering a dream*. Once again, the more spontaneous and lifelike your mental images become, the more likely you will be to move directly into a dream without losing conscious awareness.

Dream Alert—Be advised that this is not a simple process for most people. In our experience, most people who successfully achieve the state of high lucidity do so only with continued practice. Even if you don't immediately find yourself moving directly into dream lucidity from a waking state, for now it is sufficient to simply learn and practice the basic technique. If, by some chance, you do achieve a state of high lucidity tonight, we advise that you passively witness the dream without attempting to influence it in any way. You can only handle so much at once.

Dream Alert—As with more basic lucid dreams, you may fall backward into high-lucid dreams from the semiconscious state you often find yourself in during the early hours of the morning. To adapt this technique for high lucidity, simply focus on any residual mental images or dream memories. Then practice allowing yourself to fall backward into your dreams while maintaining a state of conscious awareness.

Dream Alert—As usual, practice recalling your dreams in the morning, and record the results in your dream journal.

DAY 18

WINDS OF CHANGE

On Day 18 you will continue to explore your potential for high lucidity. You will also learn an advanced version of the dream weaving technique first presented on Day 13.

Begin by choosing a new video or television program to play for at least an hour. Once again, begin this exercise about an hour before you would normally go to bed, and use a room where you can follow it through directly into a full night's sleep without being disturbed. Watch the program you've chosen for about thirty minutes, absorbing the images and enjoying the show. Then roll over, close your eyes, and enter a state of alert relaxation while concentrating on the sounds of the television in the background.

As you become increasingly relaxed, give yourself permission to have a lucid dream. As you did before, focus on remaining alert as the images in your mind become more and more spontaneous, eventually turning hypnagogic in nature. Then do your best to follow these images directly and consciously into a lucid dream.

As soon as you notice that you're having a lucid dream, study the immediate dream scenario. Remind yourself that every detail in your dream is the product of your unconscious creativity, memories, and imagination. Indeed, not only have you created the most general aspects of your dream setting, but also the tiniest and most specific details, from the architectural design of a particular dream building to the number of books on a dream shelf.

As you observe your lucid dream, pay special attention to the weather. Chances are that in this dream, as in most dreams, the weather is something you would ordinarily take for granted. Consider, however, that the weather in your dream most certainly expresses something symbolic about your present state of mind.

Now that you've noticed the weather, focus all of your energies on deliberately changing it. If you're experiencing a sweltering summer afternoon in downtown Los Angeles, for example, concentrate on making it snow. If you're lost in the middle of some dream desert, consider the possibility of invoking a heavy rain. Even if your dream takes place in a house, there's nothing except the boundaries of your imagination, as Rod Serling would have said, to prevent you from creating a thunderstorm within its walls. And even if your dream takes place underwater, you might still decide to summon a gentle spring wind.

As you deliberately alter the weather in your lucid dream, notice how the new climate both reflects and influences your underlying mood. By learning to consciously influence the weather in your dreams, you will have taken an important step toward custom-designing broader aspects of your lucid-dream scenarios. You will also have learned a simple method for assessing, in symbolic terms, the underlying atmosphere of your own psychological state. Perhaps most important, you may use this technique as a means of deliberately influencing your state of mind as you dream. You might invoke a thunderstorm, thus expressing anger, or calm yourself by creating a gentle dream rain. You might even stimulate your potential for self-healing by envisioning yourself absorbing the nurturing rays of the sun, or burning out a fever in an active volcano.

Dream Alert—As soon as you wake up in the morning, record your dreams in your journal, paying special attention to the weather within. Take special note of the relationship between your dream weather and your moods. Make this weather report a special part of your dream journal notations for the remainder of the Creative Sleep Program.

Dream Alert—Remember that the dream weaving technique takes practice and may at first result in the termination of a particular dream. If this occurs, just continue to change the dream weather in your semiconscious imagination. At the same time, practice falling backward into a lucid or high-lucid dream.

DAY 19

SHIFTING SANDS

On Day 19 you will continue practicing the skills required for high lucidity. You will also continue to gain further control over the details in your lucid dreams.

By now, you should be ready to generate hypnagogic imagery on your own, without the assistance of a television playing in the background. Therefore, begin Day 19 by lying on your back in bed and entering a state of alert relaxation.

Since you'll once again be following this exercise directly into a full night's sleep, you should begin about an hour before your usual bedtime. This time, instead of focusing on a television playing in the background, focus your attention on any hypnagogic images that emerge as you're falling asleep.

In most cases, these images will emerge spontaneously, without conscious assistance. If this does not happen for you shortly after closing your eyes, the process may be helped along by pulling up random memory fragments from experiences you had earlier in the day. Think about some of the interesting things you've encountered during the course of your day, and imagine them interacting in some surrealistic fashion in your mind. For instance, you might imagine that chicken wing you had for lunch sprouting a mouth and eyes and starting a conversation with your car radio.

As you feel yourself becoming increasingly relaxed, give yourself permission to have a lucid dream. Then continue to remain alert while observing the hypnagogic images in your mind, doing your best to follow them directly and consciously into a lucid dream. Remember, if you lose consciousness before entering a dream, you can still follow the instructions below as soon as you become aware that you're dreaming. You may also "fall backward" into a lucid or high-lucid dream upon first awakening.

Once you find yourself in a lucid dream, observe your immediate dream surroundings, taking particular note of the weather. Then imagine a compelling place completely different from the one represented in your dream. If your dream opens up on a city street, for example, you might imagine a clearing in the forest. If your dream opens on a Tibetan mountaintop, you might conjure the Brooklyn Bridge.

When you've thought of a suitably compelling location, concentrate on transforming the original setting of your dream into the new dream environment. This time, instead of spinning your dream body to turn your present dream surroundings into a shifting blur, just close your eyes while focusing on the new locale. With practice, you should be able to will your original dream setting to dissolve, while the new setting emerges in its place.

Continue practicing this exercise until you've managed to experience at least one recognizable change in your lucid-dream environment by a simple expression of conscious free will. Then observe the prevailing weather conditions of your new dream surroundings, and practice the exercise you learned on Day 18 for consciously changing your dream weather.

Dream Alert—If you happen to wake up as you shift your dream scenario, continue the exercise in your semiconscious imagination.

Dream Alert—Remember to record your dreams in your dream journal, taking special note of shifts in dream weather and locale. Consider the possible psychological and symbolic significance of your dream scenarios, and record these as well.

DAY 20

TRADING PLACES

On Day 20 you will gain a deeper understanding of the characters populating your dreams. At the end of Week One, remember, you learned to question your dream enemies, thus gaining insight into some of the demons plaguing your unconscious mind. This evening you will deliberately trade places with your dream characters to gain even more direct insight into the significance of their presence in your dreams.

Once again, begin by trying to enter a state of high lucidity from waking consciousness. If you do not succeed, induce a lucid dream later in the night with techniques learned in Week Two.

This time, when you find yourself in a lucid or high-lucid dream, pay particular attention to any characters you may encounter. If you happen to be alone at the start of your lucid dream, go for a walk, swim, or fly around until you come across some other life form. Whatever the appearance of this life form, be it Wonder Woman, the Cheshire Cat, or the Blob, there can be no doubt that its presence is a function of your own unconscious creative processes. As dream researchers have long pointed out, every character who appears in your dreams—even those who play the part of familiar figures from your everyday life—expresses some aspect of your inner self. Put simply, *you* play the part of every character in your dreams. It is therefore within your power to consciously shift perspectives with any of your dream characters.

For tonight's exercise, pick out an interesting lucid-dream character and imagine how your dream experience might appear from the other character's perspective. Imagine yourself actually trading places with this character and then looking back at the character you were previously playing in your dream. What would your new dream self say to your old dream self about the scenario you're presently experiencing? How do your feelings about yourself and your dream shift when you take on the viewpoint of the other character?

Continue practicing this exercise until you've managed to experience at least one role reversal in the course of your lucid dream. You may then either practice consciously changing perspectives and taking on the role of additional dream characters, or just opt to complete the dream from the new character's perspective. You may even decide to return to your original character, tapping any insights you may have gained from your role-reversal experience.

> **Dream Alert**—If you feel yourself waking up in the middle of this exercise, complete at least one role reversal in your semiconscious imagination. Then, if possible, allow yourself to fall backward into a lucid or high-lucid dream.

> **Dream Alert**—Record your role-reversal dreams in your dream journal, taking special note of any insights you may have gained by trading places with various dream characters. Record all other high-lucid, lucid, and ordinary dreams as well.

DAY 21

FREE DREAMING

On Day 21 of the Creative Sleep Program, we recommend another night of "free dreaming," which, as you remember, is dreaming without either deliberately influencing the content of your dreams or consciously inducing lucidity. Tonight, give your mind a chance to freely express itself while taking a break from some of the more consciously structured dreaming exercises of the past two weeks.

If you should find yourself spontaneously entering a lucid dream at some point during the night, just relax and enjoy it while assessing any subjective changes that may have emerged in the quality and intensity of your dreams over the past three weeks.

Dream Alert—As usual, record your dreams in your journal when you first wake up in the morning.

And how about celebrating with a special breakfast? You've just completed Week Three of the Creative Sleep Program.

WEEK THREE HIGH LUCIDITY

DAY 15 ALTERED STATES	DAY 16 THE ADVENTURES OF GUMBY		DAY 17 HIGH LUCIDITY
In the morning, recall and record your dreams.

With the assistance of a friend, enter the altered state of alert relaxation.

Throughout the day, assert your desire to have lucid dreams.

Read instructions for Day 16.

Before you drift off to sleep at night, enter a state of alert relaxation and assert your desire to have lucid dreams. | In the morning, recall and record your dreams.

Throughout the day, assert your desire to have lucid dreams.

Choose an appropriate television program or video.

In a room where you can eventually go to sleep without being disturbed, watch the program. After thirty minutes, close your eyes, enter a state of alert relaxation, and allow images induced by the audio portion of the program to emerge from your imagination. | After fifteen minutes, resume a state of alert waking consciousness.

Watch a bit more of the program.

Enter a state of alert relaxation, reaffirm your desire to have a lucid dream, and fall asleep. | In the morning, recall and record your dreams.

Throughout the day, assert your desire to have lucid dreams.

Choose an appropriate television program or video.

In a room where you can eventually go to sleep without being disturbed, watch the program. After thirty minutes, close your eyes, enter a state of alert relaxation, and allow images induced by the audio portion of the program to emerge from your imagination. |

	DAY 18 WINDS OF CHANGE		**DAY 19** SHIFTING SANDS
Focus on the images you see in your mind, and, maintaining a state of conscious awareness, follow these images into a high-lucid dream. If you are unable to accomplish this, induce a lucid dream as the night goes on.	In the morning, recall and record your dreams. Throughout the day, assert your desire to have lucid dreams. Choose an appropriate television program or video. In a room where you can eventually go to sleep without being disturbed, watch the program. After thirty minutes, close your eyes, enter a state of alert relaxation, and allow images induced by the audio portion of the program to emerge from your imagination.	Focus on the images you see in your mind, and, maintaining a state of conscious awareness, follow these images into a high-lucid dream. If you are unable to accomplish this, induce a lucid dream as the night goes on. Once you realize you are dreaming, attempt to change the weather in your dream.	In the morning, recall and record your dreams. Throughout the day, assert your desire to have lucid dreams. After you climb into bed, enter a state of alert relaxation. Focus on the images you see in your mind, and, maintaining a state of conscious awareness, follow these images into a high-lucid dream. If you are unable to accomplish this, induce a lucid dream as the night goes on.

(continued)

WEEK THREE   HIGH LUCIDITY (continued)

DAY 19 SHIFTING SANDS	**DAY 20** TRADING PLACES		**DAY 21** FREE DREAMING
Once you find yourself in a lucid dream, observe your immediate surroundings. Then, through sheer will, change this environment into one that seems entirely different. Observe the weather in your dream, and change that as well.	In the morning, recall and record your dreams. Throughout the day, assert your desire to have lucid dreams. After you climb into bed, enter a state of alert relaxation. Focus on the images you see in your mind, and, maintaining a state of conscious awareness, follow these images into a high-lucid dream. If you are unable to accomplish this, induce a lucid dream as the night goes on.	Once you find yourself in a lucid dream, pay particular attention to life forms populating the dream. Throughout the night, change places with one or more of the characters in your dream.	In the morning, recall and record your dreams. Go about your day much as you did before you started the Creative Sleep Program. Go to bed without doing any special dream exercises at all.

WEEK FOUR

CREATIVE CONSCIOUSNESS

WEEK FOUR

•

CREATIVE CONSCIOUSNESS

During the first three weeks of the Creative Sleep Program you've learned how to induce and sustain lucid dreams, how to change dream weather and dream locale, how to converse with dream entities, and how to travel the dream terrain. You've also learned how to incubate dream solutions to real-life problems.

In the last week of the Creative Sleep Program you will learn how to take these techniques to new heights as you apply the methods of creative consciousness to your dreams. By creatively exploring and developing your deeper lucid-dream potential, you should gain an increasingly powerful awareness of your inner self. In the process, you may also improve your creative, sexual, and professional endeavors in the waking world.

Toward this end, you will begin Week Four by learning to invoke a dream therapist, the imaginary embodiment of all the memories and experiences you've had since you were born. By assisting you in tapping the wellspring of your inner life, your dream therapist should be able to offer you some surprisingly candid and straightforward input about how you're handling your relationship with the everyday world. The dream therapist exercise will be followed by an exercise for invoking a dream healer, called upon to aid in boosting your immune system and managing your health.

Week Four exercises will also take you beyond yourself. You will learn how to share lucid dreams with friends and lovers, and as you develop your skills, how to experience incredible dream sex. Indeed, using the Creative Sleep exercises, you will learn to enact dozens of forbidden fantasies in your dreams.

Finally, in the culmination of the Creative Sleep Program, you will learn to seek higher, deeper, and potentially more profound inner experiences in your dreams. Can lucid dreamers intuit information unavailable through ordinary or explainable means? Can they learn to explore out-of-body experiences, in which their physical and mental selves seem to exist on two separate planes? From a sense of timelessness to a feeling of connectedness with a greater reality, the potential for transcendence will be revealed to those who wake up in their dreams.

DAY 22

DREAM
THERAPIST

Some of us pay our psychotherapists thousands of dollars a year just to help us clarify our thoughts and put into proper perspective things that, in the deepest recesses of our mind, we already know. Tonight you will learn to call upon the higher wisdom of a therapist in your dreams. Invoking this personal dream guide, you should gain access to information hidden in the furthest reaches of your unconscious mind.

To prepare for tonight's dream session on the analyst's couch, spend the day observing your relationship with the world. How do you interact with other people? How is your mood influenced by your surroundings? How do you react to different types of weather, traffic, and noise? How do you feel about your life and yourself? Can you chart the ebbs and flows of your moods as you go through the day?

Sometime during the day, find a quiet place where you can sit and reflect upon the condition of your personal life. Where are you at this point in your life, especially in relation to the fantasies you had as a child? Are there any recurrent themes or ideas that have motivated you as you've grown older? Are there any psychological blocks or other obstacles that have prevented you from achieving all you'd once dreamed of accomplishing? Allow your thoughts to come and go easily without holding on to them too tightly or analyzing them too closely.

Now imagine what it would be like to have a personal confidant and therapist who completely understands your innermost thoughts and feelings, and could also offer you remarkable insights into overcoming any difficulties you currently face. Imagine in as much detail as possible exactly what such an individual would look like. Would your confidant be a wise old woman with flowing gray hair, a middle-aged male psychiatrist in a three-piece suit, a hard-boiled detective from a thirties movie, or a giant white rabbit named Harvey? Would this individual wear perfume, carry a briefcase, smoke fat cigars, or consume a constant supply of fresh carrots? Imagine yourself sitting with your "therapist" in this moment, exploring your most personal feelings. Continue with this part of the exercise for at least half an hour before going about the rest of your day's activities.

Begin the next part of this exercise about an hour before you plan to go to bed. Gather together a small number of incubation objects that symbolize some significant aspects of your own life history. You might, for example, choose your baby shoes, a photograph of yourself as a child, a diploma, an old love letter, your Congressional Medal of Honor, and a religious or spiritual symbol. While you're at it, choose one additional object that expresses some recurrent concern in your personal life—a tattered valentine to represent seemingly constant troubles in romance, for instance, or an uncashed payroll check to symbolize your ongoing confusion about where you're going in your career. Place these objects on your lucid-dream altar while quietly contemplating their personal significance. You can also enhance the atmosphere by burning incense and playing music in the background.

When you're ready, get in bed and take out your dream journal. Then create an incubation phrase that expresses some overall concern you have about the current state of your life. For this exercise, don't just focus on narrow concerns, such as your perpetually confusing relationship with your boyfriend, Melvin. Instead, direct your attention toward more global concerns, such as the generally troublesome ongoing history of all your sexual relationships, of which Melvin is just the latest example. Instead of just writing, *Do I really love Melvin at all?* this time write something like, *Why do I always seem to wind up with shallow, egotistical, insensitive, ill-mannered, unfaithful slobs like Melvin?* Then turn out the lights, relax, and go to sleep.

Once again, you may attempt to enter the state of high lucidity directly from waking consciousness using the techniques practiced during Week Three. Or you may use any of the other lucid-dream induction techniques that you've explored during the previous three weeks. No matter which approach you use, however, you should focus on the concerns expressed in your incubation phrase as you're falling asleep. You should also focus on your need to gain special insights into the way you are handling your life.

We suggest that you allow your unconscious mind to provide you with a suitable dream scenario for exploring your concerns. your main focus should be to seek out a dream therapist to assist you in gaining insight into your waking life.

Toward this end, as soon as you find yourself in the midst of a lucid dream, look around for the therapist you envisioned earlier in the day. Don't worry, however, if you don't encounter this individual right away. Just explore your dream environment in any way that seems appropriate to the setting—on foot, by car, or through dream whirling or dream flight. Continue to explore until you come across the individual you're seeking. And remember, once your unconscious mind has added its input, your dream therapist may not look exactly like the individual you consciously imagined.

When you encounter your dream therapist, you may use the opportunity to seek advice and insights into your life in the waking world. Since your therapist is the embodiment of all the memories and experiences residing in your conscious and unconscious mind, he, she, or it should have access to the most intimate details of your life. Therefore, your dream therapist should be able to offer you some surprisingly candid and straightforward input about how you're handling your personal existence. Put simply, your inner self may know more about what's good for you than your conscious self is willing or able to admit. By meeting this inner self in the form of a personal therapist or guide in a lucid dream, you may be able to consciously benefit from the hidden wisdom of your unconscious mind. The more often you practice this exercise, the more incisive your insights should become.

Dream Alert—Don't worry or feel pressured if you don't meet your dream therapist the first time you practice this exercise. In any event, chances are that the dream you have incubated will express your unconscious thoughts and feelings about the concerns you focused on during the day. With continued practice you may eventually learn to meet with your dream therapist on a regular basis. You may even establish a whole society of dream therapists from a variety of lucid dreams.

Dream Alert—If you should find yourself waking up during this exercise, just continue your "therapy" in a semiconscious state.

Dream Alert—Remember that any therapist you meet in a lucid dream still exists within your own mind and is therefore not truly objective. Your inner guide is not guaranteed to provide you with omniscient insights or flawless advice, but only the potential for more direct access to the inner workings of your own unconscious mind. You should therefore rationally evaluate your lucid-dream therapy sessions in the cool light of waking reality.

Pursue only those directives that have been carefully thought out, and which can be expected to have reasonable consequences. And remember that the unconscious mind often expresses itself in symbolic ways. For example, if your dream therapist suggests, *perhaps you should consider murdering Melvin,* you would do well not to take this advice literally. Instead, you might decide to end this unhappy relationship as you begin working out your more general problems with men.

Dream Alert—If you find yourself feeling at all overwhelmed by this exercise or by any other aspect of the Creative Sleep Program, we urge you to seek out a competent real-life therapist before proceeding with the program. In our experience, however, the unconscious mind will not provide a dreamer with information that he or she is unready or unwilling to handle in waking life. Whether you choose to explore this inner source of potential wisdom on your own or in conjunction with psychotherapy in the waking world, the result can often be most beneficial.

Dream Alert—Read the instructions for Day 23 before you go to bed, and remember to record your dreams in your dream journal as soon as you wake up in the morning.

DAY 23

THE HEALER
WITHIN

On Day 23 you will expand upon the dream therapist technique by invoking the image of a personal dream healer to assist you in boosting your immune response. Today, instead of focusing on psychological concerns, direct your attention toward the overall condition of your body.

When you first wake up in the morning, begin by noticing the way your body feels as you get out of bed. Do you feel full of energy, ready to jump into the shower and bound off to work like a powerful gazelle? Or do you feel more like a hunted elephant, shot by a tranquilizer gun and fading fast? Does it take several gallons of strong black coffee to get you moving? Or is the morning sunshine and a glass of chilled orange juice enough to make you feel alive and alert?

Notice the kind of relationship you have with your body as you go about your day. Do you purposely avoid even the slightest opportunity for exercise and gorge yourself with junk food? Do you smoke? Or do you maintain a macrobiotic diet and typically spend your evenings at the health club sipping tomato juice, taking aerobics class, and lifting weights? In short, what is your attitude toward your body? How is this attitude reflected in your diet, dress, and general level of physical activity?

As you did during the last exercise, find a quiet place where you can relax for thirty minutes during the day and consider the current state of your health. Are there any chronic health problems that have troubled you for many months or years? What about other health concerns that may have begun troubling you only recently? Do you think of yourself as generally robust or as a more or less sickly individual? Allow your thoughts about your physical health to come and go easily without holding on to them or analyzing them too closely.

Now imagine what it would be like to have a personal healer who constantly monitors your physical health and assists you in taking care of your body. What would such an individual look like? A primitive tribal witch doctor in full regalia? An elderly surgeon with a white coat and stethoscope? Or Raquel Welch, clad in leg warmers and tights? Picture yourself sitting with your imaginary healer, describing your personal health history from childhood on. Continue with this part of the exercise for at least thirty minutes before going about the rest of your day.

As you did on Day 22, begin the next part of this exercise about an hour before you plan to go to bed. Choose an incubation object that symbolizes some significant concern about the current state of your physical health. You might, for example, choose a giant bag of greasy potato chips to symbolize concern over your diet (don't make the problem worse by eating them!), or an old shoe to symbolize problems with your feet. Place the object on your lucid-dream altar, and quietly contemplate its symbolic significance. Again, you might consider enhancing the atmosphere by burning incense and playing music in the background.

When you feel ready, get in bed and express your most pressing health concern in your dream journal. You might, for example, write, *How can I lose fifty pounds?* or *What can I do about my allergies?*

Then turn out the lights, relax, and use any of the techniques you've learned over the past weeks to induce a lucid or high-lucid dream. As you're falling asleep, focus on your incubation phrase and your general thoughts about your body.

Once in the midst of a lucid dream, focus on finding your dream healer, much as you focused on finding your dream therapist. When you do finally encounter this individual, seek advice about your most pressing physical concerns.

Remember, your dream healer represents a symbolic bridge between your conscious and unconscious mind. He, she, or it may therefore help you communicate with yourself at a deep inner level about the steps you need to take to improve your physical condition. If this were all this exercise was good for, however, the dream healer would be little more than a very specialized version of the dream therapist. In fact, the real potential of the dream healer exercise actually begins where the dream therapist technique leaves off.

To experience the greatest potential benefit from your dream healer, you might request a symbolic remedy for some physical problem. For example, your dream healer might lay their hands on some part of your dream body to offer you some "healing energy." Your healer might also offer you medicine or guide you to some healing environment, such as a warm salt sea, where you can envision yourself immersing your body and thriving in the healing rays of the afternoon sun.

> **Dream Alert**—Don't worry if you do not meet your dream healer the first time you practice this exercise. Your incubated dream should still provide you with insights, drawn from your own unconscious, into the way you've been approaching your physical health. If you wake up before you've finished the exercise, just complete it in a semiconscious state.

In an advanced version of this exercise, you may even serve as your own dream healer, directly incubating therapeutic dream scenarios. Indeed, a mounting body of scientific evidence shows that such creative visualization may exert a powerful influence over your immune system by assisting you in mobilizing your inner defenses and boosting your psychological response to disease. To mobilize your body's immune system in this way, first find an appropriate symbol for the offending illness or disease and place it on your lucid-dream altar! If you suffer from migraine headaches, for instance, you might imagine the symptoms in the form of a twisted, overgrown weed. You could then envision digging up such a weed in a nearby lot or park. Before you go to bed, write in your dream journal, *Tonight I will overcome my headaches in my dreams,* and focus on that idea as you fall asleep. Once you find yourself in a lucid dream seek out the weed and somehow destroy it: You might, for instance, kill it with poison gas, blow it up with dynamite, or chop it to pieces with an axe. Of course, if your problem has a primarily *emotional* basis, we recommend that you approach it in a less aggressive fashion dealing directly with your emotional problems first.

Alternatively, you might simply use this advanced method to try to boost your immunity to disease. For instance, you might envision your immune cells as tiny seeds. At night, in your lucid dream, you can generate imagery in which these seeds grow into lush, healthy plants.

Dream Alert—According to much recent research, this advanced technique can be extremely effective in boosting general energy and increasing resistance to disease. It may also be used to mobilize your defenses against a wide range of ailments from colitis to allergies to cancer. However, we suggest that if you have cancer or some other very serious illness, you practice these techniques only with the help of a guided imagery professional referred to you by your personal physician or a nearby teaching hospital, and in conjunction with all recommended medical treatments.

Dream Alert—Whether you invoke the image of a dream healer or use straightforward guided imagery to boost your health, we caution you to evaluate the input of your dream healer in the light of common sense. Under no circumstance should you ever use this exercise to replace conventional medical or psychiatric treatment. Dream healing may, however, help you respond positively to such treatment, thereby providing an additional line of psychological defense against disease.

Dream Alert—Record your dreams in your dream diary when you wake up in the morning.

DAY 24

DOUBLE VISION

One of the most profound experiences two people can share is a mutual dream. Such occurrences are actually more common than you might imagine and can create feelings of deep inner communion between those involved, as though they have somehow been together in an alternate reality or have shared an inexplicable "psychic" experience. In fact, the explanation for shared dreams is probably much more mundane, though this certainly doesn't diminish their impact. Since dreams are so directly influenced by experiences in the waking world, two people who have many waking experiences in common are also eventually likely to share the general content or subject matter of at least some of their dreams. No doubt, this is particularly the case when the individuals concerned are involved in an unusually close relationship, such as that of sexual partners, best friends, or close co-workers.

When such people share lucid dreams, the impact can be particularly profound. A shared lucid dream may allow two people to explore various issues in their relationship from a deeper perspective, or at least an alternative one. What's more, it can strengthen the inner connection between them.

On Day 24, therefore, you will practice shared dream incubation with a partner. If at all possible, your partner for this exercise should be another participant in the Creative Sleep Program. If this is not possible, your partner should at least be a close personal friend, if not a lover.

Begin the day by swapping some clothes or other personal articles with your partner. She might wear your tie as a sash, for instance, and you might wear her scarf or hat. Trading colognes or perfumes would be effective as well. Spend as much time with your friend as possible during the day, aiming for a setting rich in sensory and emotional stimulation. You might, for example, spend some time collecting fossils by the ocean, dancing at a discotheque, or riding all the elevators in your local downtown area. You might also just go out to an exciting movie, though you should be sure and pick one that is highly stimulating; a George Lucas film would be a more appropriate choice for this exercise than a film by Ingmar Bergman. If moviegoing is your choice, we also recommend that you see the film in a lively, dynamic section of town where audience participation is high—the Forty-second Street area of Manhattan fits the bill, as does the Venice area of Los Angeles. For this exercise, please avoid theaters in suburban multiplexes or malls.

Sometime in the course of your shared activity, you and your friend should each select a dream incubation object from the immediate environment. To make the selection more interesting, you should then trade objects, so that each can focus on the other's object before going to bed. You should also, when the opportunity naturally presents itself in the course of your conversations, periodically remind each other that you both intend to include elements of your shared waking experiences in tonight's dreams. Depending upon the nature of your relationship and personal predispositions, you might enhance your waking experience still further by discussing some special concerns in your private lives, entering the altered state of alert relaxation together, or simply making love.

For the purpose of this exercise, it makes no difference whether you and your partner sleep together or separately. Before turning in for the night, however, you should each take some time to reflect on your shared waking experiences, and on the incubation objects you've given each other. You should also try to wear some article of your partner's clothing to bed, and perhaps their favorite cologne as well.

Before going to sleep both you and your partner should

record in your dream journals your intention to have lucid dreams about each other. (If your friend does not currently keep a dream journal, he or she can just use a piece of paper or notepad for tonight.)

As you fall asleep, you can use any of the Creative Sleep techniques to induce a lucid or high-lucid dream. Then search the dream landscape for your friend via walking, driving, flying, or whirling, much as you searched for your dream therapist on Day 23. When you do find your friend, you may have the greatest shared adventure that dream reality has to offer. You may also use the dream to bring your relationship to new levels of intimacy, honesty, or intensity; your dream relationships, after all, can withstand large doses of these elements even when they are forbidden in everyday life.

> **Dream Alert**—When you wake up, make sure to record your dreams in your dream journal. Then compare notes with your friend. How similar or different were your two dreams? Did you experience that intensely compelling mutual experience, the shared dream? Indeed, did the two of you establish enough empathy and resonance during the day to walk the same road again in your dreams?

DAY 25

DREAM LOVERS

The exercises for Days 25 and 26 are entirely sexual. If you feel at all uncomfortable about doing these exercises, simply skip over them and spend the time brushing up on any of the previous exercises in the Creative Sleep Program. In addition, the exercise for Day 25 requires a consenting adult sexual partner, while Day 26 does not, so you may also feel free to skip today's exercise and practice the techniques described for Day 26 two days in a row. Read the instructions for both of these exercises before beginning, so that you won't have to interrupt your sexual experiences to refer to the directions.

On Day 25, spend as much time as possible thinking about and expressing your sexual and emotional connection with your partner. To start with, you and your partner should have a romantic meal, either eating enough to sustain you through today's exercise or having food and drink available throughout your lovemaking session. Be careful to keep it light: you don't want to feel full and thus inhibit your sexual activities. You can even incorporate the food itself into the exercise. We would suggest sensuous foods such as mild but tasty cheeses, Kalamata olives, Belon oysters, stuffed grape leaves, rich and creamy pastries, a large bowl of ripe fruit such as cherries, and some nice wine or fruit juice. (Naturally, you'll want to keep all of this within the confines of any dietary restrictions.) We suggest that while you're eating, you and your partner spend the time touching each other and talking about sex.

Specifically, we would like you to discuss what you plan and desire for the session of sexual abandon to follow. For instance, you might say, *I want to lick every inch of your body,* or *I crave light, painless scratches over the surface of my skin,* or *Let's pretend we're primal sensuous cave dwellers—troglodytes—without any formal language, meeting suddenly on a prehistoric beach in a storm.* Do you like wearing leather? Do you love the feel of a vibrator? Whatever your fancy, express it verbally, now.

After you've finished eating, take a sexy bath or shower together, slowly soaping each other all over and touching each other in special, sexual places. Then spend at least two hours massaging each other's naked bodies with warm, scented oil, touching, hugging, and kissing each other, and passionately making love. You might also enhance the atmosphere by playing sexy music, lighting candles, or burning incense.

Pretend you've just met your partner and that you're both discovering each other sexually for the first time. Focus on those aspects of your partner's sexuality that most excited you when you first got together. Think about the first time you saw each other naked, the first time you looked closely at one another's sexual organs, and the first time you touched each other between your legs. Remember what it felt like when your partner's sexual organs touched yours for the first time. Feel free to discuss these memories with each other. Take this opportunity to be as open with your lover as possible. Forget about the outside world—the world outside your bedroom— and for now, just concentrate on each other.

Pick out some favorite sexual thing to do, such as slowly stroking your partner into increasingly powerful multiple orgasms or taking your partner's sexual organs in your mouth and bringing him or her to climax. Then think of some equally exciting thing for your partner to do to you. Next, try something different, something you haven't done together before, such as tickling your partner with a feather or covering your lover's sexual organs with warm butterscotch syrup, steak juice, or wine and slowly licking it off.

You should be prepared to make love together until you are both exhausted and ready to fall into an easy sleep. But a few minutes before you're ready to fall asleep, before you've even stopped making love, you should start to discuss the mutual lucid dream you will incubate together. Is there a particular fantasy you'd like to act out, one that you'd never be comfortable fulfilling in real life, such as including someone else in your lovemaking, or dressing up in costumes and playing different roles? Is there a particular place you'd like to make love—the Metropolitan Museum of Art, the top of Mount Everest or the Eiffel Tower, or the cargo bay of the space shuttle? Discuss these fantasies openly, and don't be afraid to let your discussions lead into more lovemaking. Just be sure to establish some sort of goal for your mutual lucid-dream scenario. Take a minute to record your lucid-dream goal in your dream journals. (If your partner does not have a dream journal, he or she can use a page in yours, or a piece of paper.) Then continue making love until you both fall asleep.

As you fall asleep in each other's arms, focus on achieving high lucidity using the techniques described in Week Three. If this proves too taxing after your passionate evening, induce a lucid dream using any of the other methods described in the Creative Sleep Program. Also focus on fulfilling as much of your lucid-dream fantasy as possible.

As soon as you recognize that you're dreaming, look around for the dream image of your partner. If you do not see your partner, search the dream terrain, or simply will him or her to appear. Once you have found your partner, focus on fulfilling your sexual fantasy with them in your lucid dream. Use advanced dream weaving capabilities to adjust the scenery and props, from the breeze blowing the curtain to the Dom Pérignon champagne to the golden sparkles in your hair. As you carry out your intentions with your dream lover, you may find yourself experiencing the most exciting sex and the most unbridled passion of your life.

Dream Alert—The very first time you practice this exercise, you may or may not experience a full-scale sexual encounter. But even the first time out, you will more than likely have some kind of sexual dream experience. Practicing this approach on a regular basis should help you explore your sexual fantasies in your dreams. Perhaps more important, the dream lovers exercise should help you and your partner improve your sexual relationship in the waking world as well.

Dream Alert—If you find yourself moving toward waking consciousness while practicing this exercise, just continue to act out your fantasy in your semiconscious imagination.

Dream Alert—Record your dreams in your diary as soon as you wake up in the morning, and before you compare your own experiences with your partner's. Then not only tell your partner about any sexual dreams you may have had, but also consider acting out certain aspects of those dreams with them in waking reality. After practicing this exercise and reviewing your dream experiences together, you and your partner should share some low-key nonsexual activity—like playing Scrabble or going for a walk in the park—to maintain a sense of balance and reaffirm your waking connection.

DAY 26

FORBIDDEN
FANTASIES

Begin Day 26 by thinking about your sexual fantasies. Do you have any favorite scenarios—perhaps even "forbidden" fantasies—that you'd love to act out, but just would never have the nerve to follow through with in real life? Are there any past sexual encounters you'd like to reexperience right now if you could? Would you like to be making love with your current sexual partner but are unable to because the two of you are physically separated? Or would you like to experience sex with the current centerfolds in any number of popular men's or women's magazines? How about your boss, your secretary, your neighbor, your spouse's best friend, or your best friend's spouse? How about your favorite stars from stage and screen? These people may be out of reach or out of bounds in real life, but not in your lucid dreams.

Whatever your fantasy, think about it whenever you can during the day. Then, during some quiet part of the day—your lunch hour, perhaps—choose a spot where you can just sit and let your sexual fantasy run through your mind in rich and luxurious detail for the next forty-five minutes. During this period, you should focus on your fantasy until it seems palpable and real. Conjure the image of your fantasy partner in your mind. What is he or she wearing? How does he or she walk? What does it feel like to meet your dream lover in this unexpected setting so far from their home?

After you have fixed these details in your mind, imagine that the central figure of your fantasy has decided to join you for lunch. Now imagine how the conversation might go: *What are you doing here? . . . Weren't you supposed to be on the set in Cairo today? . . . Aren't you David Letterman?* As the lunch period progresses, create a full-blown fantasy in your mind. For instance, David Letterman might be lunching near your office in downtown Fayetteville just to get away from the stress of the late-night scene. He hopes no one will recognize him, but when you do, he confesses years of inner angst. Needless to say, you end up at the Fayetteville Hilton—for weeks on end. Whether the object of your secret desire is David Letterman or someone else, imagine yourself slowly undressing this person, touching your lover's naked body all over, and feeling your lover respond and touch you in return. Remember, you must fill in the details—all of them—until the forty-five-minute period has come to an end. Then go about your day, allowing your fantasy to run easily through your mind.

Carry out the next part of this exercise in your bedroom, about half an hour before you would normally go to bed. Place a symbol of your erotic fantasy on your dream altar, and write a phrase about this fantasy in your dream journal. Then get into a sexual frame of mind: you may want to put on some loose-fitting, sexy clothes, play some romantic music in the background, and drink a nice glass of fruit juice or wine.

Enter a state of alert relaxation, and focus on the sorts of thoughts, feelings, and images that you personally find most erotic. It may be helpful to think about the last time you had an intense orgasm. What were you thinking about at the time? Were you with anyone? What *exactly* were you doing at the moment of your sexual release? Now relax and recall the fantasy you enjoyed earlier in the day. Again, imagine yourself slowly undressing the object of your desire. See and feel yourself touching your lover's naked body as your lover touches you in return. Imagine the two of you in a special place together, like a romantic cabin in the woods, an old-fashioned hotel room on the Left Bank in Paris, or a secluded office at the place where you work. In this secret spot, imagine the two of you doing "forbidden" things. Enjoy the fantasy as you become more and more deeply relaxed, and, using the techniques you learned during Week Three, focus on entering the dream state of high lucidity. If you prefer, you may also allow yourself to drift off to sleep while using any of the Week Two techniques to incubate a lucid dream.

Dream Alert—Please remember, you should strive for dramatically heightened sexual arousal *without* the experience of orgasm prior to falling asleep. In this way, you will maximize the power of your desire to fulfill your fantasy in your lucid dream. Even though you will be focusing so much of your attention on your sexual fantasies throughout the day, therefore, *it is important that you avoid having an orgasm for at least twelve hours before practicing this exercise.*

Once you find yourself in a lucid or high-lucid dream, of course, you're free to follow through on your fantasy with total abandon. Remember, dream travel and dream weaving techniques can help take you anywhere in the dream world, with anyone. Have as many orgasms as you like, with whomever you like, doing whatever you like—nobody but you will ever know the difference.

Dream Alert—If you should start to wake up during this exercise, continue your fantasy in the semiconscious state while allowing yourself a sexual release.

Dream Alert—Record your dreams in your dream journal as soon as possible after you wake up.

DAY 27

EXTENDED
AWARENESS

The possiblity that dreams provide access to an extended level of awareness, one that takes the dreamer *beyond* his or her internal reality, has fascinated dream enthusiasts for as long as recorded history. Many people believe that dreams may sometimes provide information about future or far distant events, or that they may even allow two individuals to communicate directly in their sleep. In many instances, the apparent expression of such information may be explained as a product of the dreamer's imagination or as mere coincidence. Often, seemingly psychic dreams may also be explained as the unconscious integration of sensory and analytic information currently available to the dreamer through known channels.

There are some questions, however, that scientists are still asking. Can dreamers report information to which they have absolutely no access through ordinary means? And if so, can lucidity or high lucidity make it easier for dreamers to tap this mysterious expanded realm?

On Day 27, you will carry out an informal experiment to see whether your own lucid dreams can lead to extended awareness. This informal experiment is based on the work of psychiatrist and dream researcher Montague Ullman and his colleagues, who tested extended abilities in the Dream Laboratory at Maimonides Medical Center in Brooklyn, New York, during the sixties. As a result of these fascinating studies, described by Ullman and associates in the classic book *Dream Telepathy,* the Maimonides team reported strong evidence for extended awareness in dreams. Tonight you will adapt the basic experimental technique developed at Maimonides for yourself.

Begin by asking a friend to concentrate on a fifteen-minute segment of a video film before he or she goes to sleep and again just before he or she wakes up in the morning. Please ask your friend to choose a video sequence he or she is as sure as possible you have never seen, and one that contains striking audio and visual imagery. *Journey to the Center of the Earth, Dr. Strangelove,* or even a rock video like Michael Jackson's *Thriller* would work well. If watching a videotape isn't possible, just ask your friend to select a powerful magazine picture—*Life, Omni, National Geographic, Smithsonian* often have appropriately riveting shots—and to use that for this exercise. Be sure the magazine issue your friend chooses is one you've not yet seen, and that he or she chooses a photograph likely to be unique to that particular issue. After your friend chooses the video or picture, you should have no further contact with each other until you have completed the next phase of this exercise.

Go about the rest of your day as usual, conducting reality

checks and reaffirming your desire to have a lucid or high-lucid dream. Also tell yourself that the image your friend has chosen will appear in your dream. Then, before you go to sleep, tell yourself to dream about the video or photograph upon which your friend will be concentrating, and reaffirm your intention to have a lucid dream. Remember while dreaming to search the dream terrain for the images you desire. You may scan for them on a dream flight or simply will their presence with advanced dream weaving techniques.

Dream Alert—As soon as you wake up in the morning, record your dreams in your dream journal. For this exercise, it is particularly important that you draw your impressions as well. We suggest that you fill two or three pages of your dream journal with visual impressions of the kind of images you believe your friend has chosen, as well as visual impressions of any related or unrelated dreams. Once you have recorded these notes, you and your friend should get together as soon as possible. Your friend should then show you the video or photograph he or she focused on in the morning and before going to bed. Are there any similarities between your dream recollections and the material your friend was observing? Share your written impressions and drawings, and see what your friend thinks as well.

Dream Alert—As an especially interesting variation on this informal experiment, ask your friend to mix the photograph or video clip that they actually used for the exercise with a random collection of other equally interesting but very different films or pictures that weren't a part of the experiment. Then, while your friend waits in another room, see if you can pick out the correct video or photograph, based upon your remembered impressions of the previous night's dreams. Of course, this will not be a formal experiment, among other reasons because your friend will have handled the photographs or videos before you see them. But this exercise is intended for your personal interest and exploration, rather than for publication in a scientific journal. If you are motivated, you will no doubt come up with many fascinating variations on the informal experiment suggested here. We wish you every success in these endeavors.

Dream Alert—We caution you to remember a point made long ago by Sigmund Freud: even dreams that seem to suggest extended awareness no doubt also reflect that which the unconscious psyche finds most relevant. In other words, a dream cannot be discounted even if it appears on the surface to have more to do with someone else's immediate waking experience than with your own. Whether or not you believe that your dream represents an instance of extended awareness, please be sure to analyze its content in terms of its symbolic and emotional significance to *you.*

DAY 28

SATURDAY NIGHT, AIN'T GOT NO BODY

In simplest terms, the out-of-body experience, or OBE, is the subjective sensation that your awareness is temporarily located outside of your physical body. You may have had an OBE yourself, waking up in the middle of night to the perception that you have left your body lying on the bed below and are floating above it. Or you may have heard one of the numerous reports made by those who say that in the wake of a highway accident or heart attack they temporarily left their bodies.

OBEs are so fascinating and intricate that we have produced an entire book, *Have an Out-of-Body Experience in 30 Days: The Free Flight Program,* to help you explore and deliberately induce OBEs. One basic exercise that you can begin practicing tonight, however, involves inducing an out-of-body experience from the midst of a lucid dream.

Here is an appropriate place for us to point out that the OBE and the lucid dream are *not* one and the same. Though the two are often confused with each other, laboratory studies show they are psychologically and physiologically distinct. For one thing, you don't have to be asleep to have an out-of-body experience. For another, the brain wave and eye movement patterns that have emerged from OBE studies in the laboratory are quite different from those associated with dreams.

Nonetheless, one excellent way to induce an out-of-body experience is through the vehicle of the lucid dream. That technique is what you will learn today.

To begin, set aside a quiet period of about an hour during your day to visit a uniquely identifiable environment that stimulates all of your senses. You may, for example, spend some time sitting in the lion house at your local zoo, walking through an orchard full of ripe peaches, or picking through the garbage at the nearest dump. Be creative. Don't just go someplace where you're used to spending a lot of time, like your favorite bar or the downtown mall. Instead, think of someplace more unusual, like your city's science museum, or an open-air fish market.

Find a comfortable spot in the place you've chosen where you can sit down. Close your eyes for five or ten minutes and listen to the layers of sound all around you—the larger, more distant sounds, like airplanes, screams, and sirens, and the smaller, more immediate sounds, like voices in a passing crowd, or flies landing on your lunch. Keeping your eyes closed, take a deep breath and notice the smells in your surrounding environment. Does the lion house smell like wild game? Does the atmosphere of the open-air market smell like fresh fish? Is someone burning garbage at the dump? Breathe deeply and take it all in, at the same time consciously distinguishing as many different smells as you can.

With your eyes still closed, notice the way your body feels as you sit. Is the ground soft and giving, like a sand dune? Or is it hard and bumpy, like an old park bench? How does the inside of your mouth taste at this moment—fresh and minty like a stick of spearmint gum, or more like that slice of garlic pizza you had for lunch?

Open your eyes and slowly look around your immediate environment. What is the first, most striking image you see? Notice the layers of light and color in your nearby and more distant surroundings. Look up at the sky, and notice the weather. Look down and notice any shadows or patterns of light moving across the ground. Continue this part of the exercise for twenty or thirty minutes, then get up and go about the rest of your day as you normally would.

Go to sleep at your usual time, using any technique you prefer to induce a lucid or high-lucid dream. Before turning out the lights, get out your dream journal and create a phrase expressing your intention to have an OBE. Though we do not necessarily believe that OBEs represent a tangible separation of consciousness from the physical body—we simply don't have enough conclusive scientific evidence one way or the other—you may want to write a phrase like *Tonight I give myself permission to leave my body*. In this way, you'll consciously distinguish your intention for this evening from that of merely having an ordinary flying dream.

When you practice this exercise, you may find that merely making a conscious decision to allow yourself to have an OBE is enough to trigger the experience. More likely, however, is the possibility that you will simply find yourself having a lucid dream, perhaps one involving elements of the place in which you practiced the sensory awareness exercise earlier. In any event, as soon as you recognize that you're dreaming, turn your attention toward your real body—not your image of your body participating in the dream scenario, but your physical body lying in bed. Don't worry about maintaining your lucid dream. Instead, allow your dream images to quietly drift into the background of your awareness, or to fade altogether from your mind.

As you are doing this, it is crucial that you do not open your eyes, move, or allow yourself to return completely to waking consciousness. Ideally, this technique will engender a state between lucid dreaming and waking, a state in which everyday physical reality seems to take on some of the flexible dimensions of a dream. Allow yourself to briefly maintain this somewhat distanced and surrealistic perspective toward your body. Then turn your attention entirely toward your memories of the spot in which you practiced the sensory awareness exercise earlier in the day.

Remember how it felt to sit with your eyes closed at that

distant location, and imagine you are back there now, experiencing those same feelings once again. Conjure all your impressions of that distant locale, from the sounds to the textures, the smells, and the most striking visual images of the day. Allow these impressions to fully crystallize in your imagination, until you almost feel as though you are present in that distant place. As this feeling intensifies for you, imagine yourself floating around the distant environment, experiencing it from a variety of shifting perspectives. If your images are powerful enough, you may induce an authentic OBE. Finally, when your desire to "travel outside the body" has been sated, and when you feel comfortable doing so, focus once more on your feelings toward your body.

When you turn your attention back toward your body, do you find yourself once again experiencing images from your lucid dream? If so, simply allow yourself to return directly to the dream state and continue with the rest of your night's sleeping and dreaming experiences. If not, just allow yourself to concentrate on what it feels iike to be lying in bed, and gradually allow yourself to awaken or fall back into sleep.

How will you know whether you have had a real OBE, were just imagining things, or merely dreaming about having such an experience? Good question! Unfortunately, in the absence of your own home monitoring equipment and a couple of physiologists, the question is difficult to answer. We therefore suggest that you consider this: an actual out-of-body experience is so subjectively striking when it occurs that it should distinguish itself from any other type of experience you may have had. In other words, having an OBE is like having an orgasm or falling in love. When it happens, you usually recognize it.

> **Dream Alert**—If you don't have an out-of-body experience the first time you practice this exercise, there's no need to pressure yourself or feel concerned. With years of lucid dreaming ahead of you, there should be many opportunities for you to practice this exercise in the future. If you are particularly intrigued, as we are, with the fascinating realm of OBEs, consider checking out *Have an Out-of-Body Experience in 30 Days: The Free Flight Program*.

Dream Alert—Remember to record your dreams or out-of-body experiences in your dream journal as soon as you wake up in the morning.

WEEK FOUR CREATIVE CONSCIOUSNESS

DAY 22 DREAM THERAPIST		DAY 23 THE HEALER WITHIN	
In the morning, recall and record your dreams.	Express your concern in your dream journal.	In the morning, recall and record your dreams.	Express your concern in your dream journal.
Spend the day observing your relationship with the world.	Induce a lucid or high-lucid dream.	Spend the day observing how you feel about your body.	Induce a lucid or high-lucid dream.
Imagine a personal therapist or confidant who could help you solve your problems.	Navigate the dream environment until you find your dream therapist, and see what he or she has to say.	Imagine a personal healer who could help you achieve optimum fitness and health.	Navigate the dream environment until you find your dream healer, and see what he or she has to say. Ask your dream healer to assist in healing you.
About an hour before you go to bed, gather a few objects that represent your life history, as well as an object that symbolizes an ongoing problem, and place them near your lucidity symbol.		About an hour before you go to bed, choose an incubation object that symbolizes some significant concern about your health. Place it near your lucidity symbol.	

DAY 24 DOUBLE VISION		**DAY 25** DREAM LOVERS	
Go home and place the object your friend has given you beside your lucidity symbol.

Record your intention to dream about your friend in your dream journal.

Think about your friend as you fall asleep.

Induce a lucid or high-lucid dream.

Search the dream landscape for your friend. | In the morning, recall and record your dreams.

Recruit a friend with whom to share this exercise and part of this day.

Swap some clothing with your partner.

Share a day or part of a day doing something memorable.

Discuss your intention to dream about each other.

Each find an object symbolizing your time together.

Trade objects. | In the morning, recall and record your dreams.

Compare notes with your friend.

Recruit a lover with whom to share this exercise and part of this day.

Have a romantic meal, and discuss your plans for a session of sexual abandon to follow.

Take a bath or shower together.

Spend two hours making love.

Discuss the mutual dream you would like to incubate together. | Record your goals in your dream journals.

Continue making love. Then fall asleep, inducing a lucid or high-lucid dream.

When you realize you are dreaming, seek out your partner in the dream.

Adjust the dream scenery and props for romantic effect.

Carry out the sexual intentions you discussed before you fell asleep within the context of the dream.

(continued) |

WEEK FOUR   CREATIVE CONSCIOUSNESS (continued)

DAY 26 FORBIDDEN FANTASIES		DAY 27 EXTENDED AWARENESS		
In the morning, recall and record your dreams. Think about your own sexual fantasies. At some point during the day, go alone to a quiet spot and imagine a sexual encounter with the dream lover of your choice. Place a symbol for your erotic fantasy next to your lucidity symbol. Get into a sexy state of mind. Enter a state of alert relaxation and think about your sexual fantasy.	Induce a lucid or high-lucid dream. Follow through on your fantasy with total abandon within the context of the dream. Compare notes with your partner of Day 25.	In the morning, recall and record your dreams. Recruit a friend, and ask him or her to choose a stimulating video sequence or photograph and focus on it for fifteen minutes before going to bed and again after getting up in the morning. Throughout the day, stop and ask yourself whether or not you are dreaming. Throughout the day, assert your desire to have lucid dreams.	Tell yourself that the image your friend has chosen will appear in your dream. Before you go to sleep, tell yourself to dream about the image upon which your friend has focused. Reaffirm your intention to have a lucid dream. Induce a lucid or high-lucid dream. Once you find yourself dreaming, search the dream terrain for the images you must identify.	

DAY 28
SATURDAY
NIGHT, AIN'T
GOT NO
BODY

In the morning, recall and record your dreams. Today, make a special effort to draw pictures of your impressions as well.

Visit your friend and view the images he or she chose to focus on the night before.

Throughout the day, stop and ask yourself whether or not you are dreaming.

Throughout the day, assert your desire to have lucid dreams.

Visit a special, extremely stimulating locale.

Sit, close your eyes, and listen to the sounds around you.

Notice the smells.

Notice the way your body feels.

Open your eyes and look around.

After you go to bed, get out your dream journal and record your intention to have an out-of-body experience.

Induce a lucid or high-lucid dream.

As soon as you realize you're dreaming, try to focus on your sleeping body.

As your dream images fade, remember the spot you sat in during the day.

Focus on that distant locale until you feel as if you are having an out-of-body experience.

Turn your attention toward your body once more and fall back to sleep.

•

T O W A R D   H I G H E R
C O N S C I O U S N E S S

*T*here is a moment upon just waking up from a dream when you experience a startling shift in perspective; in that moment you realize that the life you were most recently leading—the life in your dream—was merely a product of your imagination. In this transition period your return to the waking world often seems like the termination of an illusion. As you must realize by now, moreover, awakening from a lucid dream can be just as startling. That's because the conscious realization that you are dreaming does not dilute the power of your dream identity at all.

In one of our all-time favorite dreams, the dreamer found himself in an amusement park, confronting a magnificent roller coaster with a sign that read LIFE. The dreamer took a seat in the front car and handed his ticket to the roller coaster operator. "Ready to go?" the operator asked the dreamer. "You know, it's a hell of an illusion!"

"I'm sure I can handle it," the dreamer said, "I've been on this ride before." With this, the ride commenced. The scenario of the amusement park faded, and the dreamer found himself being born as an infant in another reality. Before long, the dreamer saw himself growing up, going to school, graduating, developing a career, getting married, having a family, growing old, and eventually dying. All of this seemed to cover a life span of roughly seventy or eighty years. As the dreamer finally felt his life fading away, he heard the sounds of the roller coaster slowing down in the background. In a moment, he found himself back in the amusement park, looking up at the operator from his seat in the front car.

"Well," the operator asked him. "How was it? Learn anything?"

"That was pretty incredible," the dreamer said, suddenly aware that he was experiencing this alternate reality in a dream. Now thoroughly lucid and hoping to take the dream further still, he handed the operator another ticket. "This time," he said, "I'd like to be someone else." The roller coaster started again, and the dreamer immediately woke up. Needless to say, upon awakening from this dream the dreamer could not help but wonder whether he was returning to an absolutely tangible reality or was experiencing yet another convincing illusion.

The dreamer came away from this dream somehow changed; the moment of awakening jogged something in his mind so that he experienced a sense of expanded consciousness. The illusory nature of his dream helped him understand something profound about the illusory nature of his own waking life. Moreover, the dreamer felt more comfortable with the concept of death. Indeed, he viewed it more than ever as part of the larger, cosmic scheme of things—something he could, in effect, transcend. Perhaps most important, he recognized in his dream identity a deep and long-hidden part of his inner self.

Indeed, lucid dreamers who spend a great deal of time merely manipulating their dreams may eventually lose sight of their greater potential: to consciously explore the unconscious, thus getting a better grasp of what they want in life and of who they are.

On Days 29 and 30 of the Creative Sleep Program, you will embark upon a journey toward higher consciousness. Your goal will be to explore the shift in perspective you undergo as you wake up, turning from an imaginary character in dreamland into your everyday self. By doing so, you can literally carry the lessons of your dreams into your everyday life, becoming a more fulfilled and self-aware version of the person you truly are. In the process, you may also gain insights into philosophical dilemmas ranging from the nature of reality to the meaning of death to the concept of God.

On Day 29 of the Creative Sleep Program conduct reality

checks during the day as you usually do and from time to time reaffirm your desire to have a lucid dream. For a thirty-minute period during some quiet part of the day, consider the things that make you uniquely you. Do you wear big floppy hats? Blue mascara and aquamarine contact lenses? A giant fur coat you bought from the Salvation Army in 1972? Do you make love at midday in the office rest room, or have a penchant for mayonnaise on your salami sandwich for lunch? Do you hang posters of John Travolta on your bedroom wall? Whatever your quirks, whatever your specialties, review them now. When the thirty-minute period has ended, drop this line of thought and go about the rest of your day.

Just before you go to bed, write in your dream journal, *Let my deepest self find expression in my dreams*. Then turn off the light and use any comfortable method to induce a lucid or high-lucid dream. Whenever you recognize that you are dreaming, pay particular attention to the way you feel toward the identity you have assumed within the dream. Ask yourself, *Who do I seem to be now?* Notice the way your sense of yourself subtly shifts when you focus on this question. Instead of attempting to change elements in your dream just for fun, allow your dream personality to explore the rich and varied environment your subconscious has seen fit to create. See that dirt road down there? Instead of changing it to a superhighway, just follow it. If along the way you see a mountain range, climb or fly over it to see what lies beyond, and if you pass a house by the side of the road, take the opportunity to go inside. If the house harbors a witch, listen to her incantation, and if you can, tell her about your life as an entity in a dream.

Remember, dream weaving techniques are best approached only as an aid to greater discovery. Instead of deliberately changing a particular dream prop, scene, or character, for instance, you may call upon your dreams to alter themselves. In this way, their symbolic meaning may become especially clear.

You might, for example, turn toward the image of Godzilla chasing you through the dream ruins of Tokyo and ask, in any way that seems appropriate, *Who or what are you and where the hell am I?* As you express this thought, your dream images might actually "weave" themselves into a form that makes their meaning clear. Does Godzilla ravaging Tokyo turn into an image of your mother kicking over your blocks in your room when you were three? Or does the famous Japanese monster turn into a fleet of shiny new Toyotas devastating your Chevy dealership? As your dream symbols come clear, you will realize they represent yourself, your job and your family, as well as your concepts of death, reality, and God.

As you navigate the dream terrain, remind yourself that you are in the midst of your own, self-induced illusion, and that a much broader reality exists beyond the veil of the dream. Do not be concerned if turning your attention toward such thoughts has the effect of terminating a particular lucid dream, since the next part of this exercise is meant to be practiced immediately upon awakening from such an experience.

In the moment that you notice yourself returning to consciousness, repeat the question that you asked yourself in the dream: *Who do I seem to be now?* Remember the way you felt about yourself in your most recent dream, and compare that experience with your sense of yourself in this moment. Look around at the everyday world, and ask yourself if there may be a broader reality, however you wish to define this concept for yourself, beyond the limits of your ordinary perceptions. Is this other reality a deeper, more vibrant realm that you simply cannot perceive from the waking state, just as you cannot perceive waking reality while in the midst of a dream?

Continue asking yourself these questions from time to time throughout Day 30: *Who do I seem to be now? Is there a broader reality beyond my everyday perceptions?* Also think about the dream exploration you conducted the night before; focus especially on the moment of transition between sleep and wakefulness.

You will bring this exercise to its conclusion on the last night of the Creative Sleep Program, when, if you are fortunate, you will attain a sense of transcendence, and a deeper understanding of the waking world. Before you go to bed, consider what the experience of transcendence might include for you: a sense of connectedness with something greater than your individual identity; a feeling of timelessness that blurs the distinction between past, present, and future; a feeling of profound meaningfulness, in which you experience insights into the nature of reality and existence; a sense of religious reverie; or simply a sense of objectivity toward mundane concerns. Also remember the last time you felt such feelings in a deep and profound way.

Then, right before you go to sleep, draw a picture—any related picture that comes to mind—in your dream journal. Finally, focus on that drawing as you induce a lucid or high-lucid dream. Remember to seek those special feelings of transcendence as you explore the rich dream terrain. In this way, you can call upon the wisdom of your inner self to provide you with a transcendent lucid dream. Remember to note how your sense of reality shifts in the moment that you wake up. In that moment, also consider the universe that might be beckoning from beyond the limits of your senses—if the veil of ordinary reality could only be swept away.

We hope you will continue practicing the exercises you've learned over the past thirty days, and that you will continue to explore and enjoy the world through your lucid dreams. We suggest that you spend the next few nights taking a break and allowing yourself some time for free dreaming, as you did on Days 14 and 21. Then continue to adapt the Creative Sleep techniques in the ways best suited to you. In the meantime, congratulations are in order. You've just completed the Creative Sleep Program!

APPENDIX A

•

A SPECIAL NOTE
TO THE
PHYSICALLY
DISABLED

*F*or the sake of simplicity, the instructions for many of the exercises in the Creative Sleep Program appear to assume certain basic physical capabilities. We sincerely hope, however, that the Creative Sleep Program will attract a diverse readership, including many individuals who may have any of a wide variety of physical disabilities. In fact, there is absolutely no reason why the techniques presented in the Creative Sleep Program cannot be practiced by everyone.

In much of our research at the Institute for Advanced Psychology, disabled individuals have made a significant contribution to our exploration and understanding of a wide range of extended human capabilities. We therefore request that our disabled readers bear with us, and that they feel free to adapt the various Creative Sleep exercises to their personal capabilities and preferences.

We suggest, for example, that if you are blind, hearing impaired, usually in a wheelchair, or otherwise restricted in your ability to easily move around your environment, that you simply adjust the exercises to your particular needs; we assure you that the program will work just as well. We also remind you that many of the Creative Sleep exercises are easily adaptable to a wide variety of available sensory and psychological approaches. If necessary, it is completely acceptable to skip a particular exercise, simply replacing it with another more suited to your requirements on a particular day. It is also always acceptable to proceed at a pace that feels most comfortable for you and works best in your individual situation.

We thank you for your interest and participation in the Creative Sleep Program. We hope it will add a new dimension of enriching inner exploration and experience to your life.

—Keith Harary and Pamela Weintraub

APPENDIX B

•

FOR FURTHER READING

Delaney, Gayle. *The Hidden Language of the Heart: Unlocking the Secrets of Your Dreams*. New York: Bantam, 1989.

Delaney, Gayle. *Living Your Dreams*. New York: Harper & Row, 1979.

Domhoff, William. *The Mystique of Dreams: A Search for Utopia Through Senoi Dream Theory*. Berkeley: University of California Press, 1985.

Evans-Wentz, W. Y. (Editor). *Tibetan Yoga and Secret Doctrines*. London: Oxford, 1958.

Faraday, Ann. *The Dream Game*. New York: Harper & Row, 1974.

LaBerge, Stephen. *Lucid Dreaming*. Los Angeles: Jeremy P. Tarcher, Inc., 1976.

Michael, Mary, and Barbara Andrews. *Dreams and Waking Visions*. New York: St. Martin's Press, 1989.

Morris, Jill. *The Dream Workbook: Discover the Knowledge and Power Hidden In Your Dreams*. Boston: Little, Brown & Co., 1985.

Ullman, Montague, M.D., Stanley Krippner, and Alan Vaughan. *Dream Telepathy*. New York: MacMillan, 1973.

ACKNOWLEDGMENTS

We wish to express our sincere gratitude to our spouses, Darlene Moore, who first showed herself in a dream, and Mark Teich, who appears in dreams all the time.

We would also like to thank our colleagues and friends who helped us explore the scientific, clinical, and personal meaning of dreams, especially those whose suggestions and research we have drawn upon in developing the Creative Sleep Program. First, our very special appreciation to Dr. Gayle Delaney for her remarkable acumen in the field of dream interpretation. Our further appreciation to Dr. Ann Faraday, Dr. Jill Morris, Dr. Jayne Gackenbach, Joel Kramer, Dr. Diana Alsted, and Dr. William Domhoff.

Special thanks also goes to our insightful and talented editor, Robert Weil, who came up with the thirty-day concept and encouraged and cajoled us through our work on this project. We would also like to express gratitude to Bill Thomas and Julia Pastore of St. Martin's Press, for their input and for the cordiality that has made working on this book such a pleasure. Finally, we would like to express our appreciation to our literary agents, Wendy Lipkind and Roslyn Targ.

We also extend our appreciation to the board of directors and board of scientific advisors of the Institute for Advanced Psychology for their role in furthering advanced psychological research.

—Keith Harary and Pamela Weintraub

ABOUT THE AUTHORS

KEITH HARARY, Ph.D., has spent decades investigating the issues confronting those who are coping with extraordinary experiences. His research has included extensive laboratory and field research on the physiological and other variables associated with altered states of consciousness, including the development of specialized methods for actively inducing a wide range of altered states.

Harary holds a Ph.D. in psychology, with emphases in both clinical counseling and experimental psychology. He has authored or co-authored hundreds of articles and eight books on topics related to perception, altered states of consciousness, personality, and related topics. He is currently Research Director of the Institute for Advanced Psychology in Tiburon, California, where he continues to conduct research in perception and other areas in association with an interdisciplinary consortium of scientists.

PAMELA WEINTRAUB is a longtime magazine journalist living in New York City and the author of thirteen books. She was formerly the editor-in-chief of *Omni*.